READING JAPANESE SIGNS

READING JAPANESE SIGNS

Deciphering Daily Life in Japan

Ian McArthur

KODANSHA INTERNATIONAL
Tokyo•New York•London

Distributed in the United States by Kodansha America, Inc., 114 Fifth Avenue, New York, N.Y. 10011, and in the United Kingdom and continental Europe by Kodansha Europe Ltd., 95 Aldwych, London WC2B 4JF.
Published by Kodansha International Ltd., 17-14 Otowa 1-chome, Bunkyo-ku, Tokyo 112, and Kodansha America, Inc.
First edition, 1994.

94 95 96 97 98 10 9 8 7 6 5 4 3 2 1

Library of Congress Cataloging-in-Publication Data

McArthur, Ian
Reading Japanese signs: deciphering daily life in Japan / Ian McArthur.—1st ed.
    p.   cm.
ISBN 4-7700-1671-9
1. Japan—Social life and customs—1945– 2. Japanese language—Terms and phrases. 3. Signs and signboards—Japan.
I. Title.
DS822.5.M376 1994
962.04—dc20   93-27290
                                                    CIP

CONTENTS

INTRODUCTION

When I first came to Japan about twenty years ago, the written Japanese in the thousands of bright neon signs overwhelmed me. The characters were, as now, seemingly everywhere. To this day, I still wrestle with *kanji*, Chinese characters. Yet when I compare my current knowledge of Japan with what I knew on my first visit, I realize that my understanding has deepened. I believe this improvement has probably been achieved by forcing myself to read. Only through reading Japanese—whether on neon signs on top of buildings, the menu at your neighborhood restaurant, or the junk mail that lies in your letter box—do you come to terms with Japan as it really is on a daily basis.

Many foreigners do not make the effort to become familiar with the Japanese writing system. You can get by in Japan without knowing *kanji*, or even *hiragana* or *katakana*. But I am convinced that so much more can be gained, so many more rich experiences can be had, if you take even a modicum of time to learn the basics of how to read and write.

I hope that this book inspires readers to make the effort to learn Japanese. I have attempted to do this by focusing on the multitude of signs, forms, and labels that you encounter in your daily life in Japan. For once, the written Japanese that you encounter in your daily life in Japan is elucidated. It's all here: the Japanese, its romanization, English translations, and explanations.

By focusing on these items, this book answers some basic questions relating to matters of survival in Japan. How can I find a part-time job? What does my prescription say? When and where do I put the garbage out, and what do I do with the television set I don't need anymore? How can I pay my gas bill?

As a fellow foreigner in Japan, I would like to share some of my own experiences to help you come to terms with Japan. Most likely, you will confront many problems upon your arrival in Japan and even well after you have settled in. Japan doesn't have to remain a difficult or even frustrating environment once there is understanding. This book will illustrate that most of these problems can be overcome through a better comprehension of what is going on around you. For example, being able to read the menu at your local pub and restaurant gives you a chance to eat a meal out and get to know your neighbors. If you learn to read the signs at the video store, you can escape from the Japanese language for a few hours by watching a movie in English. And perhaps all the information you need to know about what to do and where to go in case a big earthquake hits your area of Japan is in your mailbox or even on the sign at the end of your street. I hope this book acts as an aid for your daily life in Japan and impresses upon you how far a little knowledge of Japanese goes.

One word on how to read the romanized Japanese words. Long vowels are indicated with a bar over the top. Thus "o" is pronounced as in the word "orange," but "ō" is pronounced as in word "boat."

I would like to thank my wife, Mari Minami, for helping me find much of the information contained in these pages, and Mr. Masanobu Matsuo for taking many of the photographs, many of them at short notice. I also owe a debt of gratitude to the library staff at the Foreign Correspondents' Club of Japan for their tireless help in locating information in their files. Finally, I would like to acknowledge the help of the Mainichi Daily News where many of the essays in this book began life as part of a regular column.

Part

1

Establishing Roots

Renting a Home

If you are a poor foreigner who has just arrived in the land of the high yen, and you have to do the rounds with the real estate agents, read on. Plenty has been written about agents and landlords who refuse to deal with foreigners. It's true. I know from experience how hard it is to convince agents and landlords that I'm not going to hold raucous parties, tear apart the bathroom, or flee the country overnight, leaving a month's rent unpaid and cigarette burns in the tatami.

A recent survey by the Osaka municipal government asked residents what they thought of people being denied accommodations because they are not Japanese. Forty percent said apartment owners have the right to decide who they rent to; thirty percent said turning foreigners away would avoid "needless inconvenience." The fact of the matter is that many Japanese still perceive renting to foreigners as something best to avoid.

So don your best clothes, brush up on your Japanese, and get yourself some name cards to hand out to prospective agents. It also pays to have a resumé written in Japanese to give to agents who begin to express some interest in you. You may find that given a resumé to study, agents will come to your side and go to tremendous lengths to persuade hesitant landlords that although you're a *gaijin-san*, you have a respectable job with the respectable company mentioned on the resumé.

Once through that hoop, you will have to pay money. Lots of it: a fee of a month's rent to the apartment finder, two months' rent as a refundable *shikikin*, or security deposit, and another two months' rent as a non-refundable *reikin*, euphemistically known as key money, to thank the landlord for being so kind as to allow you to rent a place.

ADVERTISEMENT FOR AN APARTMENT

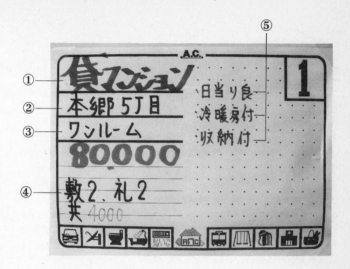

① *Kashi manshon*
Apartment for rent

② *Hongō 5-chōme*
(Location of apartment)

③ *Wan-rūmu*
One-room apartment

④ *Shiki[kin] 2, Rei[kin] 2*
2 months' rent for the deposit [money], 2 months'
rent for the gift [money]

Kyō[ekihi] 4,000
¥4,000 monthly fee for communal services
in the apartment building

⑤ *Hiatari ryō*   Good sunlight

Rei-danbō tsuki   With air conditioner and heater

Shūnō tsuki   With closets

Banks

It doesn't matter how long or short a time you stay in Japan. You are free to open a bank account anytime. Banks are open for business from Monday to Friday, from 9 A.M. to 3 P.M. If you need cash outside of those hours, make sure you get a cash card for access to your bank's automatic teller machine. These are usually open from 8:45 A.M. to 7 P.M. on weekdays, with limited service at heavily used banks on weekends, though the hours may be short. Incidentally, some banks charge a 103 yen service fee if you make a withdrawal after 6 P.M. from their machines. Most banks have agreements so their customers can use other banks' cash machines. This means if your regular bank is the Dai-Ichi Kangyo Bank, you can still walk up to a Fuji Bank cash dispenser and use your card to get your money.

For ordinary savings accounts, interest is paid twice yearly, in February and August. I find Japanese interest rates for ordinary savings abysmally low and prefer to maintain a form of a high-interest, composite account known as a *sōgō* account. This type of account combines the features of an ordinary savings, a time deposit, and a credit account.

One of the nicer ways the banks have devised for getting some extra money from transactions is the service they supply in paying our bills directly out of our accounts. It's easy. Just walk up to the counter at your bank and the teller will kindly arrange for your gas, water, and electricity payments to be automatically deducted. From then on you won't have to put up with the sight of bills cluttering your mailbox. The monthly shock will come instead when you monitor the process in your bank passbook.

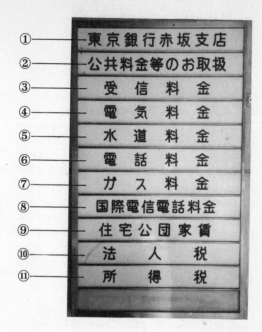

① *Tōkyō Ginkō Akasaka Shiten*
Bank of Tokyo Akasaka
Branch

② *Kōkyō-ryōkin nado no*
otoriatsukai
Public utility charges and other
services handled

③ *Jushin-ryōkin*
Television reception
payments

④ *Denki-ryōkin*
Electricity payments

⑤ *Suidō-ryōkin*
Water payments

⑥ *Denwa-ryōkin*
Telephone payments

⑦ *Gasu-ryōkin*
Gas payments

⑧ *Kokusai-denshin-denwa-ryōkin*
KDD (International Tele-
graph and Telephone)
payments

⑨ *Jūtaku Kōdan yachin*
Public Housing Corporation
rent

⑩ *Hōjin-zei*
Corporate tax

⑪ *Shotoku-zei*
Income tax

At the Post Office

Naturally, post offices in Japan perform their expected function of getting mail to its destination in good time. But they also offer a myriad of additional services such as international mail order catalogs, prepaid return postcards, a combination of a faxed letter and flowers, and musical cards.

In a pinch, I can get a few extra thousand yen from my postal savings account, even on a Sunday. What's more, the interest rate on a postal savings account is better than that offered by any bank. And unlike the banks, the post office doesn't charge a fee for using the ATM on weekends. If a relative abroad has a cash flow problem, I can send money to him or her through a mail transfer or telegraphic transfer handled by the foreign mail section of a post office. Such a transfer takes two to three days.

Last Christmas, my wife discovered one of the craziest and most charming services of the post office, mailing Christmas trees. The post office forwards your order to a Nagoya-based company which then delivers a healthy, potted tree, complete with fake snow, baubles, and tinsel. The trees are only about twenty centimeters high, but a year ago they helped bring some Christmas cheer to my wife's grandparents, living in Atami.

The post office offers additional gifts to send year-round through their *furusato kozutsumi*, hometown parcel catalog service. This service supplies fruit and other local products fresh from the prefecture where they're produced. Just fill in the order form with the name and address of the person you want to surprise.

① *Bunkyō-Mejirodai Ichi Yūbinkyoku*
Bunkyo-Mejirodai #1 Post Office

② *Tegami, hagaki*   ③ *Sonota no yūbin*
Letters, postcards   Other mail

④ *Onegai* Request

Ōki-i yūbin, sokutatsu-bin, denshi-yūbin (retakkusu) wa, subete [migi-gawa no sashiire-guchi] ni oire kudasai.
Please place large mail, express mail, and letax in the slot on the right.

15

Utilities

If you want to save yourself the bother of visiting the bank or post office to pay your utility bills, you can arrange with your bank or post office to debit the amount due from your account every month. Your gas, water, or electricity company will let you know the charge via a form which the person reading your meter will leave in your mailbox. These forms become records of your consumption.

Since the first oil crisis in the mid-seventies, Japan has promoted the diversification of power sources in an attempt to move away from a dependence on oil. There has been a consequent increase in the number of coal- and gas-fired power stations as well as nuclear power stations. Government plans call for a doubling of the currently operating forty-two nuclear reactors by the year 2010.

Japan imports around seventy percent of the world's total liquid natural gas (LNG); however, this accounts for only ten percent of the nation's energy consumption. Tokyo Electric Power Company, the largest power company in the nation in terms of sales, supplies the Kanto region with a mixture of energy sources, including coal, LNG, and nuclear power. Tokyo Electric Power Company's resources are severely strained during summer months, when air conditioners are on all over the city. Peak demand usually occurs on the hottest summer days. In the nation's capital, the situation is so tight that the electricity supply is only enough to maintain a 1.5 million kilowatt margin—or three percent over peak demand.

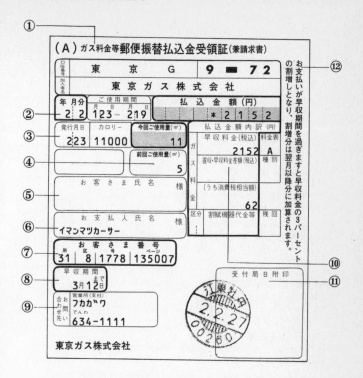

① *Gasu ryōkin tō yūbin furikae haraikomi-kin juryōshō (ken seikyūsho)*
Transfer slip for payment of gas fee through post office (bill and receipt)

② *2 nen 2 gatsu bun, Goshiyō-kikan: 1 gatsu 23 nichi 2 gatsu 19 nichi, Haraikomi-kingaku (yen): 2152*
Heisei 2 February, Period of use: January 23-February 19, Amount of payment (yen): 2152

③ *Hakkōgappi: 2 gatsu 23 nichi, Karorii: 11,000, Konkai goshiyōryō: 11m³*
Date bill was issued: February 23, Calorie: 11,000, Amount of gas used this period: 11m³

④ *Zenkai goshiyōryō: 5m³*
Amount of gas used last period: 5m³

⑤ *Okyakusama shimei: __sama*
User's name: Mr./Ms.__

⑥ *Oshiharainin shimei: Ian Makkāsā sama*
Payer's name: Mr. Ian McArthur

⑦ *Okyakusama bangō*
User's account number (at Tokyo Gas for company records)

⑧ *Sōshū-kikan: 3 gatsu 12 nichi made*
Early payment period: till March 12th (bills are to be paid during this early payment period)

⑨ *Otoiawase-saki: Fukugawa eigyōsho (shisha), Denwa 634-1111*
Inquiry center: Fukugawa sales office, Telephone number 634-1111

⑩ *Haraikomi-kingaku uchiwake (yen): Gasu-ryōkin, Sōshū-ryōkin (zeikomi): 2152, Chishū • sōshū-ryōkin sagaku (zeikomi), (Uchi shōhizei sōtōgaku:) 62, Kubun, Kappu kiki daikin tō*
Itemization of payment (yen): Gas fee, Early payment fee (tax included): 2152, Difference between late and early payment (tax included), (Consumption tax:) 62, Sector, Periods remaining for gas appliance lease fee and other items.

⑪ *Uketsuke-kyoku hizuke in*
(Stamp showing date and place where payment received)

⑫ *Oshiharai ga sōshū-kikan wo sugimasu to sōshū-ryōkin no 3 pāsento no warimashi to nari, warimashibun wa yokugetsu ikōbun ni kasan saremasu.*
If fee is paid after the early payment period, the fee will increase by 3%. This 3% penalty will be added to the next payment.

Hello Work!

Unemployed? Looking for work? If you are a spouse of a national, a permanent resident, a student, or someone who is on a cultural activities visa, go to your local ward or town *Kōkyō-Shokugyō-Anteijo*, Public Employment Security Office, now known as Hello Work Center. Those foreigners in Japan with the status mentioned above are permitted to work for a certain number of hours each week. Be sure to check with the immigration authorities about the maximum number of hours you can work. Hello Work Centers should be able to tell you but it pays to know of any exceptions, and only immigration authorities can grant exemptions.

Hello Work Centers handle inquiries from prospective employers seeking skilled foreigners for part-time and full-time positions. Centers have a computer record of vacant positions and can do a nationwide computer search if you like. An employee at my local Hello Work Center warned that an inability to speak Japanese is a major handicap; virtually all prospective employers seek Japanese-speaking foreigners.

While you are looking for a job, you might be eligible for unemployment benefits. If you are a permanent resident or spouse of a national and have paid unemployment insurance for at least six months while you were working, you should be able to apply for unemployment benefits at your local Hello Work Center.

PART-TIME WORK REQUEST FORM FOR WOMEN

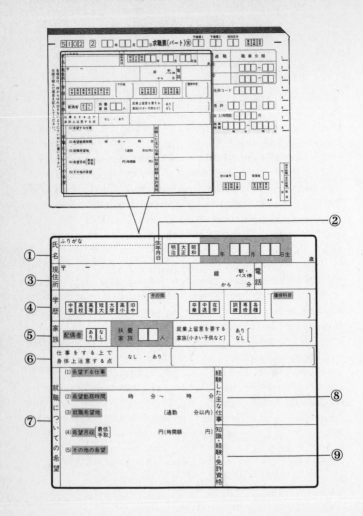

① *Shimei (furigana)*
Name (furigana)

② *Seinen-gappi: Meiji • Taishō • Shōwa, __nen __gatsu __nichi umare, __sai*
Date of birth: Meiji • Taishō • Shōwa, Born on __year __month __date, __age

③ *Genjūsho, __sen __eki • basu-tei kara __fun, denwa*
Present address, Residence is __minutes from __line __station • bus stop, Telephone number

④ *Gakureki: chūgaku • kōkō • kōsen • tandai • daigaku • kōshō • kyūchū • sonota • sotsugyō • chūtai • zaigaku • kunren •senshū • kakushu • rishū-kamoku*
Educational history: junior high school • high school • technical school • two-year college • college • pre-war junior high school • pre-war high school • graduate • drop-out • currently enrolled • technical school • special vocation skill • vocational school • trained in

⑤ *Kazoku: haigūsha ari • nashi, Fuyō kazoku __nin, Shūgyōjō ryūi wo yōsuru kazoku (chiisai kodomo nado) ari • nashi*
Family: Spouse yes • no, Dependents in family __ people, Dependent family members who may affect your work (such as children) yes • no

⑥ *Shigoto wo suru uede shintaijō chūisuru ten: nashi • ari*
Health problems that may affect your work: yes • no

⑦ *Shūshoku ni tsuite no kibō:*
Work ambitions:

1. *Kibō suru shigoto* Desired positions

2. *Kibō kinmu jikan* Desired hours

3. *Shūshoku kibōchi* Desired location

4. *Kibō gesshū (saitei tedori)* Desired salary (minimum amount after tax)

5. *Sonota no kibō* Other requests

⑧ *Keiken shita omo-na shigoto*
Previous work experience

⑨ *Chishiki • keiken • menkyoshikaku*
Knowledge • experience • license

Now Hiring

If you can answer the following three questions in the affirmative, then you could earn about 700,000 yen a month.

1. Can you drive a large truck very long distances?
2. Do you like working irregular hours?
3. Do you know how to get a truckload of apples from Aomori to a wholesale fruit market in Tsukiji in central Tokyo in the fastest possible time by road?

If you have answered all of the above with a yes, then several cargo companies are desperate to see you with a view to immediate employment. The high income reflects a shortage of people willing to do manual work.

Despite the current economic situation, part-time work is available in many sectors of the economy. In Japan, there are two forms of part-time work: *pāto*, which means limited hours of work, perhaps only in the evenings or only two days a week, and *arubaito*, which often means full working weeks and hours but without the benefits of a company employee. The job described above is an example of *arubaito*.

My own local convenience store used to stay open until 1 A.M. which is why I liked the area when apartment hunting, since I like being able to stop by around midnight for the next morning's milk on the way home from a late night's work. But soon after I moved into the area, the store began closing at 11 P.M. Now it closes at 10 P.M., and there's often a shortage of milk in the house when I get up in the morning. The supermarket manager blames it all on the lack of available staff. The store always has a sign up begging people to apply for work.

JOB ADVERTISEMENT

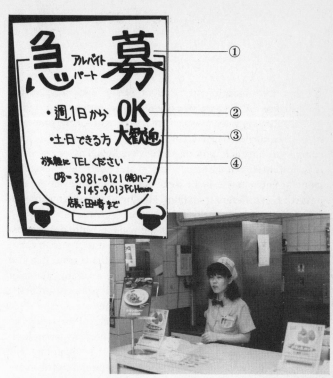

A part-time worker in a fast-food restaurant

① *Kyūbo* Hiring immediately

  Arubaito Part-time work

  Pāto Part-time work (limited hours)

② *Shū 1 nichi kara OK.*
  If you work more than 1 day a week, it's okay.

③ *Do nichi dekiru kata daikangei.*
  We greatly welcome those who can work Saturdays or Sundays.

④ *Okigaru ni tel kudasai*
  Please feel free to call.

  (Kabu) Hāfu Half Inc. *F.C. Heven* (name of the store)

  Tenchō: Tazaki made
  Please contact store manager: Tazaki

Commuter Pass

If you're commuting to work or school each day on the Japanese rail system, you'll want to equip yourself with a *teiki-ken*, a commuter rail pass. It'll save you lots of time and money. In major cities like Tokyo and Osaka, many of the train companies have computerized their wickets. Passes use magnetized film so that they easily slip in and out of the wicket machine at entry and exit. In some cases, you can even get one pass for two different train lines. Having a pass also means you can stop at any station along the route.

Most companies will compensate you for commuter expenses. My own company does this by adding it to my salary, but I'm the one who actually has to line up at the ticket office and buy the pass. Commuter passes are only available at major stations. Buying a three-month or six-month pass instead of the shorter one-month pass also saves you money.

If you're discovered cheating on a ticket or using an expired *teiki-ken*, you'll be up for a hefty fine. East Japan Railway Company has fare cheaters pay twice the proper fare. For a *teiki-ken*, the company assumes the offender used it every day, including weekends, and adds nasty penalties as well. The record in fines was paid by a man living in Tochigi Prefecture who commuted to Tokyo using a *teiki-ken* which expired on March 7, 1988, until he was caught on March 10, 1993. He paid almost 14 million yen. His method for avoiding payment was to tilt the *teiki-ken* so it couldn't be seen properly by the station workers at the entrance and exit. Don't try cheating. It doesn't work.

COMMUTER PASS APPLICATION FORM

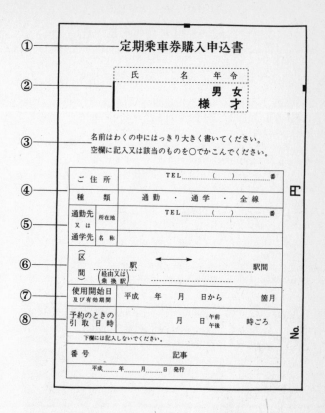

① **定期乗車券購入申込書**

氏	名	年 令
		男 女
	様	才

名前はわくの中にはっきり大きく書いてください。
空欄に記入又は該当のものを○でかこんでください。

ご住所		TEL（ ）番
種 類		通勤 ・ 通学 ・ 全線
通勤先 又は 通学先	所在地	TEL（ ）番
	名 称	
(区間)	駅 ←→ 駅間
	経由又は乗換駅
使用開始日 及び有効期間	平成 年 月 日から 箇月
予約のときの 引取日時	月 日 午前 午後 時ごろ

下欄には記入しないでください。

番号	記事

平成 年 月 日 発行

① *Teikijōsha-ken kōnyū mōshikomisho*
   Commuter pass purchase application form

② *Shimei, Nenrei, Otoko • onna, __sama, __sai*
   Full name, Age, Male • female, Mr./Ms.__, __age

③ *Namae wa waku no naka ni hakkiri ōkiku kaite kudasai.*
Please write your name largely and clearly in the box.

Kūran ni kinyū mata wa gaitō no mono wo ○ [maru] de kakonde kudasai.
Please fill in the boxes and circle the items of choice.

④ *Gojūsho* Address

Shurui: tsūkin • tsūgaku • zensen
Type [of commute]: commute to work • school • one subway line

⑤ *Tsūkinsaki mata wa tsūgakusaki: shozaichi, meishō*
Company or school to which you are commuting: address, name

⑥ *(Kukan), __eki __eki kan, (Keiyu mata wa norikae eki)*
(Section [of commute]), Between __station and __station, (Via __station or transfer station)

⑦ *Shiyō kaishibi oyobi yūkō kikan: Heisei __nen __gatsu __nichi kara __kagetsu*
First day of use or period of use: from Heisei __year __month __day, valid for __months

⑧ *Yoyaku no toki no hikitori nichiji: __gatsu __nichi gozen • gogo __ji goro*
In case of reservation, date of receiving pass: __month __day __o'clock in the morning • afternoon

A subway station entrance

Health Insurance

The national health insurance plan pays seventy percent of most of your medical bills. If you are in the country for a year or more, or if you have stayed six months and have proof showing that you'll be in the country for an additional six months or longer, you are eligible to join. Your passport to discounted medical care is the health insurance card which you can get at your ward or town office. Take your alien registration card and a school certificate or some form of identification from your place of employment when you apply. Premiums are based on your income; they can be paid at a bank or post office at regular intervals, or you can arrange with the bank to have them deducted automatically from your account. Your card should be renewed every year.

Once you have your card, remember to take it with you whenever you get medical attention at a hospital or neighborhood clinic. If you fail to present your card at the hospital or clinic, pay the full fee and then take the bill to the local ward or town office for a seventy percent refund. If you have problems paying your medical bill for unavoidable reasons, you may discuss the problem with your ward or town office officials, who might then choose to exempt you from payment, reduce the amount you have to pay, or extend the period of payment.

For those working for a large company, there is a company-affiliated health insurance plan. Instead of paying thirty percent of your medical bill, the company will pay a share of your premiums, leaving you to pay ten percent of your medical bills.

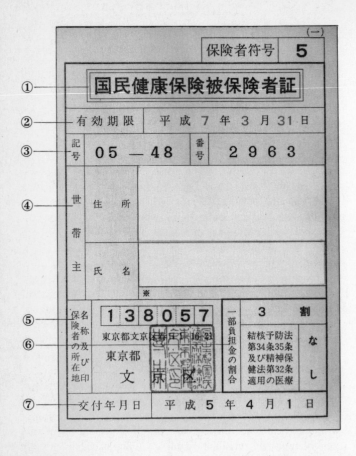

① *Kokumin-kenkō-hoken hihokensha-shō*
  National Health Insurance Card for the person
  insured

② *Yūkō-kigen: Heisei 7 nen 3 gatsu 31 nichi*
  Period of validity: Heisei 7 March 31

③ *Kigō: 05-48, Bangō: 2963*
Code: 05-48, Number: 2963

④ *Setainushi: Jūsho, Shimei*
Head of household: [his or her] address and name

⑤ *Hokensha no shozaichi meishō oyobi in: Tōkyō-to Bunkyō-ku*
Name, address, and seal of the insurer: Tokyo Metropolis, Bunkyo ward

⑥ *Ichibu futankin no wariai: san wari. Kekkaku yobō-hō dai 34 jō 35 jō oyobi seishin hoken-hō dai 32 jō tekiyō no iryō: nashi.*
Proportion of fee [paid by person insured]: thirty percent. Payment of treatment under the tuberculosis prevention law clause 34 and 35, and mental health law clause 32: free.

⑦ *Kōfu nengappi: Heisei 5 nen 4 gatsu 1 nichi*
Date of issue: Heisei 5 August 1

⑧ *Shinsatsu-chū*
Examining Patients

⑨ *Shoshin no kata wa hoken-shō wo odashi kudasai.*
If this is your first visit, please present your health insurance card.

⑩ *Saishin no kata wa shinsatsu-ken wo odashi kudasai.*
For all other patients, please present your clinic I.D. card.

⑧　　　⑨

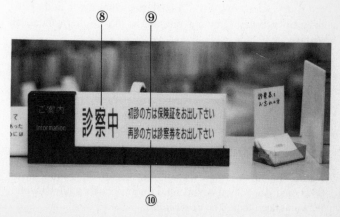

⑩

Medicine

Toyama, north of Nagoya on the coast of the Japan Sea, was once the center of medicine production in Japan. Itinerant medicine peddlers used to fan out all over the country from Toyama, making their calls to homes along their routes. Once a year, they would stop at a customer's home, sip some tea, chat with family members, and check to see which medicine in the family medicine chest had aged and become unusable. The custom still persists in some areas of Japan. In large cities, many major companies that insure their employees have adapted this custom by supplying employees with a medicine kit.

The pharmaceutical industry began in Toyama after a visiting physician from Okayama presented the area's ruling daimyo, Maeda Masatoshi, with some medicine prepared from a family recipe. Impressed by its curative powers, the daimyo ordered that the medicine be mass-produced under his auspices, resulting in fame and fortune for Toyama's medicine producers. Although producers now concentrate on Western drugs in contrast to the traditional medicines made in the seventeenth century, Toyama remains a major pharmaceutical center.

Japan's pharmaceutical manufacturers have an excellent reputation. What surprises foreigners is that doctors in Japan tend to dispense medicine more freely than in many other countries. This tendency stems from operating pharmacies as part of the clinic. Put in a better light, it could be described as "one-stop shopping": See the doc and collect your cure, all under one roof.

But having received the medicine, the task of reading the instructions remains. How many of which tablets should you take each day? Should you take them before or after meals? Will you need to get the prescription refilled?

PACKAGE OF PRESCRIBED MEDICINE

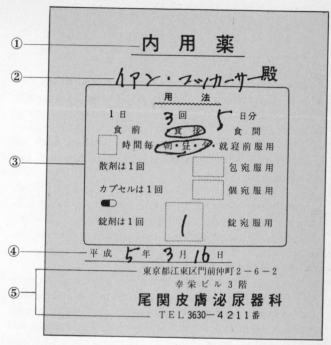

① Naiyōyaku
Internal medicine

② Ian Makkāsā dono
Mr. Ian McArthur

③ Yōhō Usage

Ichi nichi 3 kai 5 ka bun
shokuzen • shokugo • shokkan
Take 3 times a day for 5 days
before meals • after meals •
between meals.

__jikan goto asa • hiru • yū •
shūshinmae fukuyō.
Take medicine __hours, every
morning • afternoon • evening
• before going to bed.

Sanzai wa 1 kai __hō ate fukuyō
__packet per dosage

Kapuseru wa 1 kai __ko ate
fukuyō. __capsule per dosage

Jōzai wa 1 kai 1 jō ate fukuyō
1 pill per dosage

④ Heisei 5 nen 3 gatsu 16 nichi
Heisei 5 March 16

⑤ Tokyo-to Kōtō-ku Monzen
Nakachō 2-6-2 Kōei Bldg. 3 Flr.
(Address of clinic)

Ozeki Hifu Hinyōki-ka Ozeki
Dermatology and Urology
Clinic

Kids

Japan's low birth rate indicates barriers exist for raising children—the cramped living areas, absent fathers, the expense. For foreigners, the additional element of being in a foreign land can make the whole idea of having children a harrowing one. But with a bit of research and determination, many will find that having and raising children in Japan has its own special advantages.

Japan is one of the world's safest nations, with terrific public transportation to reach the various amusement parks, zoos, and aquariums. Children, for better or for worse, are held in a special light in Japan. The fact that a pregnant mother will give the only empty seat in a cramped subway car to her seven-year-old child attests to this.

Renting is a cheap and convenient way around the problem of spending millions of yen on items infants and children quickly outgrow. A friend found a rental company's free catalog in the waiting room at her gynecologist. The company had everything from party clothes to beds. You can rent a high chair for ten thousand yen for six months. Or a stroller for 15,000 for six months. Also, in the past few years, secondhand children's clothing shops have begun to spring up here and there in Japan.

If you are pregnant in Japan, register your pregnancy at your local ward or town office. In so doing, you will receive a health card entitling you to free checkups during your pregnancy and a *boshi-techō*, a mother-and-child handbook. This handbook becomes your record of health until you deliver the child, at which point it becomes the health record for your child's first six years. The *boshi-techō* is also a required document if you register your child as a Japanese national.

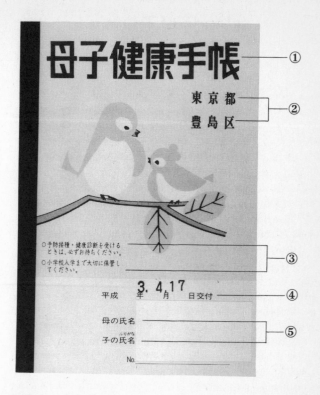

① *Boshi-kenkō-techō*
Mother-And-Child Health Handbook

② *Tōkyō-to, Toshima-ku*
Tokyo Metropolis, Toshima ward

③ *Yobō-sesshu • kenko-shindan wo ukeru toki wa, kanarazu omochi kudasai.*
Please bring this along whenever you go for a vaccination or medical check-up.

Shōgakkō nyūgaku made taisetsu ni hokan shite kudasai.
Please keep this booklet until your child enters elementary school.

④ *Heisei 3 nen 4 gatsu 17 nichi kōfu*
Issued on Heisei 3 April 17

⑤ *Haha no shimei*
Mother's name

Ko no shimei (furigana)
Child's name (in furigana)

Islands of Trash

As many a poor foreigner in Japan knows, the cost of living can be prohibitive. But one man's rubbish can be another man's living room decor. Step outside the night before *sodai-gomi* or big garbage day, as many foreigners do, and chances are you'll find just the nicest little television, bookcase, or table discarded in the rubbish heap.

Workers at Tokyo's artificial islands, where the city's garbage is rapidly piling up, say it is not even unusual these days to find functioning pianos that have been discarded by their owners. Given the space restrictions of small Japanese apartments, once an item is no longer being used, the easiest thing to do is to get rid of it. In practice, that often means the garbage dump.

To get your *sodai-gomi* picked up, call your local ward office. In Tokyo, city authorities charge a fee for taking away your *sodai-gomi*: your refrigerator will cost you one thousand yen and the television will cost six hundred yen.

Most major Japanese cities have established a system of separating garbage at the household level into burnables and non-burnables with different collection days for each. Be sure not to make the mistake of placing burnables in the bins labeled non-burnable. Many foreigners earn a bad reputation in Japan by not making the distinction, which is one reason why some landlords will not rent to non-Japanese. And don't put garbage out until the morning of its collection. Nothing irritates neighbors more than garbage sitting on the pavement for several days while the cats raid it.

① *Gomi-yōki shūsekijo*
   Trash can placement site

② *Gomi no shūshūbi*
   Trash collection days

③ *Futsū-gomi: yasaikuzu (namagomi) kamikuzu nado,*
   Ka Moku Dō
   General trash: vegetable scraps, (raw garbage,)
   scrap paper, etc., Tues., Thurs., Sat.

④ *Bunbetsu-gomi: purasuchikku, gomu, hikaku, kin-zoku, garasu, setomono, tsutsugata kandenchi, nado, Getsu*
Separated trash: plastics, rubber, hides, metals, glass, crockery, batteries, etc., Mon.

⑤ *Sodai-gomi: gomi yōki ni hairanai ōkina gomi. Mōshikomi sei desu. Denwa nado de seisō jimusho ni gorenraku kudasai. Otaku made shūshū ni uka-gaimasu node koko niwa dasanaide kudasai.*
Large size trash: large items of trash that will not fit in the trash container. Picked up on application. Please contact the refuse collection office by phone or other means. We will come to your house to collect the items, so please do not put the items out here.

⑥ *Daidokoro no gomi wa mizu wo yoku kitte dashite kudasai. Gomi-yōki niwa kanarazu futa to namae wo, itsumo seiketsu ni, shūshū ga owattara sugu hikitotte kudasai.*
Please throw away your kitchen trash after properly draining the water from it. Please ensure containers have lids and names on them; always keep containers clean and retrieve them as soon as collection is completed.

⑦ *Gomi wa kichin to bunbetsu shite dashimashō.*
Separate garbage properly before you put it out.

⑧ *Gomi no shūsekijo ni tsuki chūsha wa goenryo kudasai.*
Please refrain from parking next to the trash can placement site.

Garbage being carried to Tokyo's artificial islands

Part

2

Looking Around

Fire!

In the last century, when Tokyo was named Edo, fires earned the nickname "the flowers of Edo." Easily the largest city in the world, Tokyo's closely built wooden houses, castles, and temples were continually subject to the ravages of fire. As with the great fire of London, Tokyo, and other major Japanese cities, suffered huge conflagrations which with sickening regularity cut swathes through densely populated areas. The fires were most common in the winter months, when the air was dry and strong winds could fan the flames.

The early foreigners in Yokohama discovered the dangers posed by closely erected wooden buildings in November 1866 when a fire that had been started by an absent-minded cook in the Japanese quarter spread. Before the day was out the fire had destroyed many of the settlers' houses and warehouses near the waterfront. Only weeks later, a fire broke out in Tokyo and according to one foreign journalist at the time "…was not extinguished until such a space was cleared as led to a calculation that, had the houses and edifices destroyed been placed in a line, side by side, they would extend to a distance of 16 *ri*, or over 39 miles."

Fires remain an ever-present threat in Japan. According to the Fire Department, the main causes of fire in Tokyo are arson, cigarettes, and gas kitchen stoves. Fires caused by cooking on kitchen stoves are often started when cooking oil goes up in flames. Remember that if a fire begins, keep calm and call 119.

STREET SIGN AND DISASTER EVACUATION AREA MAP

① *Akiya ni-chōme 16*
(Location of this area)

② *Kono chiiki no kōiki-hinanchi wa Ōkusu Chūgakkō.*
Yokosuka-shi
The refuge site for this area is Okusu
Middle School. Yokosuka City

③ *Hinan basho 24 Ochanomizu Joshi Daigaku*
Shelter area 24 Ochanomizu University

④ *Riyōku Bunkyo-ku*
For use of Bunkyo-ku Ward

H w Not to Get Lost

Sure, hou s in Japan have addresses. But apart from the main i ersections, street signs are rare. Sometimes, on some block , you find street names on a wall or light pole, but decipher g what all the numbers indicate is difficult. You might s mble across a painted outdoor map of a certain area, but th r placement seems quite arbitrary and you can never tell w en they were last updated. The police have detailed map and can point you in the right direction. But just in case yo can't find a policeman, a basic understanding of how Ja an is administratively divided will help you find residences office buildings.

One *to* (*Tokyō-to*), one *dō* (*Hokkaidō*), two *fu* (*Ōsaka-fu* and *Kyōto-fu*), and forty-three *ken*, or prefectures, make up the first division, called the *todōfuken* division. Though *to* is usually translated as "metropolis" and *dō*, *fu*, and *ken* all translate as "prefecture," all forty-seven areas have equivalent administrative status. The next division consists of *ku*, ward, and *gun*, districts, followed by *machi*, town. *Machi* are then broken down into *chōme*, blocks, and *chōme* are divided into *banchi*, streets or sub-blocks. Finally the house numbers or buildings are listed. Buildings are usually numbered in the sequence by which they were originally built, not in a physically sequential order.

Of course, exceptions to these standard divisions exist. In Tokyo, a *ku*, *mura*, *shi*, and some *machi* have equivalent administrative status. Also, please note that when addresses are written, division names are often not written. Take Tokyo-to, Minato-ku, Roppongi, 3-4-12, Nishimura Jane as an example. Roppongi has the equivalent status of a *machi*; 3 is the *chōme*; 4 is the *banchi* and 12 is the house number.

STREET SIGN SHOWING ADDRESS

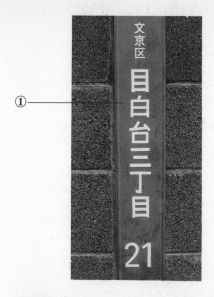

① 文京区 目白台三丁目 21

Police box in central Tokyo

① *Bunkyō-ku Mejirodai San-chōme 21*
Bunkyo-ku Ward Mejirodai 3-chome 21

Recycling Yesterday's Papers

At first it is but a faint cry in the distance, several blocks away. I strain to make out the words from the loudspeaker against the background of other city noises. Sure enough, the truck is approaching my block.

"This is your paper exchange truck. If you have old newspapers, magazines, or cloth you no longer need, we are here to take them from you. We are now slowly passing through your neighborhood. If you'd like us to stop, please let us know."

These familiar words galvanize me into action. The paper exchange truck is becoming rarer in my neighborhood as it becomes less profitable. My papers are piling up to the point where, like my neighbors, I have begun to resort to including them with the rubbish. Tokyo is now constructing another, artificial island in Tokyo Bay to cope with the current exponential growth in waste.

I rush to bundle the papers, mentally toting up how many rolls of toilet paper I might manage to receive. In the old days paper exchangers often competed for customers by offering their upper limit: four toilet rolls and a pack of tissues per household.

The pendulum has swung. These days it's the householder who is increasingly grateful just to have someone come by and take the load away. A whole street of housewives and I prepare our bundles with lightening speed, scared that the truck will roll by before we have been able to signal our need.

Just as the truck turns onto my block, the phone rings. Should I ignore the phone and risk missing an opportunity? I answer the phone; it's my mother-in-law. The paper exchange truck is disappearing around the corner. I am done for. How long will I be stuck with this growing pile of newspapers?

① *Kōkan no oshirase* Exchange notification

② *Furushinbun • furuzasshi • denwachō • boro*
Old newspapers • old magazines • telephone books • rags

③ *Ashita__nichi kuji made ni chirashi wo soete doa no soto ni dashite kudasai.*
Please attach this leaflet onto your pile of newspapers and place the pile outside your door by nine o'clock tomorrow, the __day.

④ *Tagyōsha yori gowari otoku desu.*
[Exchange rate is] fifty percent better than other operators.

⑤ *Kōkankai: toiretto pēpā • keshōshi • poketto tisshū • hako tisshū*
Exchange: toilet paper • tissue • pocket tissue packs • boxed tissues

⑥ *Uten kekkō: kodomokai • jichikai • sono-hoka • dantai • kojin*
Will take items even in rain from: children's groups • associations • other organizations • individuals.

⑦ *Kōkanristu saikō* Top exchange rate

⑧ *Eitai Shigyō* Eitai Paper Productions

Boxed Lunches

The *bentō*, or boxed meal, is a national institution in Japan. Every schoolchild is familiar with his or her mother's *bentō*, packed each morning with loving care in plastic or tin containers and opened at lunch time. Construction workers eat *bentō* for lunch. Film crews on location eat *bentō*. Kabuki audiences can choose to eat *bentō* called *makunouchi bentō*, literally "between acts" *bentō*. Single office workers pick up *bentō* on their way home at night to save themselves the bother of cooking a meal at the end of a tiring day.

All *bentō* contain plentiful helpings of rice, but it is the other ingredients in a *bentō* that give each its mark of distinction: tiny Vienna sausages with eggs that have been sweetened with sugar and scrambled, *shiojake*, salted baked salmon and seaweed, fried prawns with cooked vegetables, or *yakiniku*, grilled meat.

If you don't have time to pack your own *bentō*, you can purchase a *bentō* at a department store, convenience store, or grocery store. Chain stores such as Hoka Hoka Bento are often found around offices and student hangouts. *Bentō* prices range from about 500 to 2,500 yen.

Japan also has a tremendous variety of *ekiben*, station *bentō*, sold at train stations around the country. Pull into any station on a long-distance train journey and you will see the stands on the platform stocked with *ekiben*. On the bullet trains, railway employees hawk their *bentō* up and down the aisles, usually selling *bentō* with specialties from the places the trains are passing through. For example, Toyama by the Japan Sea has a highly praised *masuzushi bentō*, trout sushi *bentō*. In Gunma, Takasaki is known for its Daruma *bentō*, so named because it comes in a Daruma doll-shaped container.

Samples of sushi *bentō*

① *Ezo-mae*
Hokkaido style (Tohoku and Hokkaido prefectures were once called Ezo.)

② *Shiretoko*
(Name of a place that this *bentō* has been named after.)

③ *Ikura mi yama*
Three clusters of salmon roe

Kani sake
Crab and salmon

47

Fortune-telling

Years ago, a fortune-teller back home in Australia told me that I would go to an island. Could that island be Japan? Fortune-tellers abound in Japan. Mostly, you find them near train stations, from late afternoon until late evening, where they cater to those going out for the night or businessmen returning home. Their fee hovers around 3,000 yen. Although their readings may vary, fortune-tellers look fairly uniform: dressed in dark colors, sitting upright on a stool in front of a small table on which a small paper lantern stands.

My more recent attempt at seeing into the future was in the Ginza in Tokyo. I consulted a gentleman who specializes in reading palms. My reading took about six minutes, after which I was able to ask questions.

Palm reading in Japan is not too different than in the West. The creases on the palms have much the same appellations. Their significance is self-evident in their names: the *seimei-sen*, the life line, the *chinō-sen*, the intelligence line, the *unmei-sen*, the destiny line, the *kanjō-sen*, the emotion line, and the *taiyō-sen*, which indicates degrees of sociability.

In my case, I was told that the way I held out my right hand for examination, with all the fingers neatly resting together, indicated filial piety. The proximity of my second finger and middle finger indicated a good relationship with my parents. The closeness of my little finger and my ring finger indicated a good relationship with my children. My emotion line was well-defined, indicating an emotional disposition. I also had a distinct fate line, which I was told indicated future success.

"Well, after all, you are writing a book, aren't you," my palm reader said.

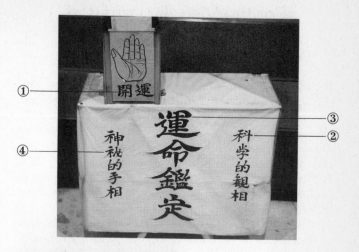

① *Kaiun* Improve your future

② *Kagakuteki-kansō*
Scientific physiognomic readings

③ *Unmei-kantei*
Fortune consultation

④ *Shinpiteki-tesō*
Mystic palm reading

For the Visually Impaired

Yellow braille blocks are found along sidewalks and railway stations in many places around Japan. These blocks assist the blind. As of 1992, there were over 800,000 braille blocks in Japan. There are two types: ones with long, straight raised bars which indicate that the path remains straight, and ones with raised dots which indicate that the path takes a turn. The Transport Ministry has specified that the braille blocks used on railway platforms be placed eighty centimeters from the edge of the platform.

The accompanying message asking the general public not to place objects on the braille blocks is apparently a necessary one. The Kanagawa Light Center in Yokohama, which is about ten minutes from the nearest station, has the blocks on the sidewalks leading to it. Despite large signs explaining the blocks purpose, the center's staff is constantly frustrated by drivers parking their cars atop the blocks. "We just wish people would understand that by parking on the blocks, they make it so difficult for people who can't see," said one employee. In such situations, the blind might have to walk on the street which puts them at risk of being hit by a car. The absence of sidewalks on many roads also makes walking in Japan a dangerous exercise for the visually impaired.

Japan has around 3 million people described as *shikaku shōgaisha*, visually impaired. The Light Center in Kanagawa is one branch of Light Centers nationwide which train the visually impaired in reading braille and other basic skills. Special primary, junior high, and high schools teach blind children standard curricula and additional skills. Many totally and partially sight-impaired people once went into the traditional trade of massage. They are now increasingly finding work in computer programming or other fields.

BRAILLE BLOCKS

（①）目の不自由な方のものです。モノをおかないで。

Training guide dogs for
the visually impaired

① *Me no fujiyūna kata no mono desu. Mono wo okanaide!*
These blocks are for the visually impaired. Do no
place objects on them.

Silver Seats

She must have been around eighty years old. The elderly woman got on the train at Shinjuku, Tokyo's busiest station. She looked exhausted, yet she retained that look of stoic endurance and dignity I have seen so many times on the faces of elderly women who would dearly love a seat, but cannot find one in the entire carriage.

The train pulled into the next station, where, nearly in front of the elderly women, a young man stood up and leapt for the exit. Calmly, and as carefully as her weary bones would allow her, the elderly woman approached the seat, turned, and slowly allowed herself to descend—onto the knobby knees of a middle-aged male office worker who had beaten her to it from halfway down the other end of the carriage. The office worker feigned indifference and promptly closed his eyes and pretended to go to sleep. The elderly woman abruptly rose from the man's lap, proffered a few mumbled words of apology, and regained her former precarious but dignified position.

This incident was before the introduction of Silver Seats, which can now be found on most national and private railway trains as well as many buses. Silver Seats are two or three seats on each train carriage or bus specially designated for the elderly or handicapped. Their different colored seats and distinctive signs found on the adjacent windows or walls identify Silver Seats. Signs on the walls of station platforms also indicate that Silver Seats can be found opposite that spot on the platform in each train passing through the station.

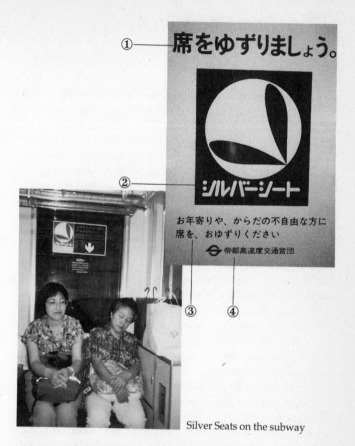

席をゆずりましょう。

シルバーシート

お年寄りや、からだの不自由な方に
席を、おゆずりください

帝都高速度交通営団

Silver Seats on the subway

① *Seki wo yuzurimashō.* Let's give up our seat.

② *Shirubā-shīto* Silver Seats

③ *Otoshiyori ya karada no fujiyū na kata ni seki wo oyuzuri kudasai.*
Let's give up our seats to the elderly and to handicapped persons.

④ *Teito Kōsokudo Kōtsū Eidan*
Metropolitan Rapid Transit Corporation

Fast Food On Wheels

After a long day at work and a commute home on a crowded train, few things could be more satisfying than a hot meal delivered to your front door. If you are single and fall ill, nothing is easier than ordering a bowl of soup to eat in your pajamas at home. And if you haven't been able to make all your side dishes for the party you are holding, having the local *sushi* restaurant deliver you a few rolls of *sushi* will get you off the hook.

An assortment of *demae*, or home-delivered foods, can be found in Japan: pizza, monster sandwiches, Chinese food, *sushi*, *soba*, and *ramen*. With the large number of *demae* services available, a *demae* meal should take no longer than thirty minutes to be delivered. Chances are you've come across a *demae* menu in your mailbox. Or you can get yourself menus from you nearby restaurants. When you pick up menus, make sure that you live within the radius of the area that the restaurant will deliver to. After finishing your meal, Japanese *demae* manners dictate that patrons rinse the plates and bowls and leave them outside their doors.

When calling the restaurant to place an order, make sure you are dialing the correct number. Though you think that you would be told if you have dialed the wrong number, you never know. A workmate's father continually gets calls for home-delivered noodles because his phone number is one digit different from that of the noodle shop nearby. He is fed up with explaining this so pretends he's the noodle shop and politely goes through the motions of taking the order. Unfortunately for the customers, he draws the line at ringing up the noodle shop and passing on the order.

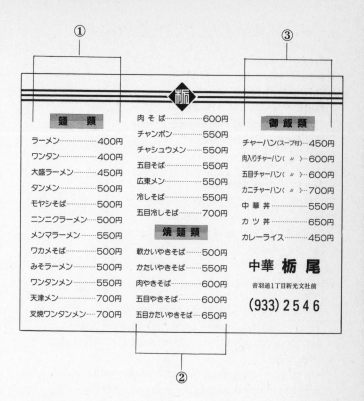

麺　類

ラーメン	400円
ワンタン	400円
大盛ラーメン	450円
タンメン	500円
モヤシそば	500円
ニンニクラーメン	500円
メンマラーメン	550円
ワカメそば	500円
みそラーメン	500円
ワンタンメン	550円
天津メン	700円
叉焼ワンタンメン	700円

肉そば	600円
チャンポン	550円
チャシュウメン	550円
五目そば	550円
広東メン	550円
冷しそば	550円
五目冷しそば	700円

焼麺類

軟かいやきそば	500円
かたいやきそば	550円
肉やきそば	600円
五目やきそば	600円
五目かたいやきそば	650円

御飯類

チャーハン(スープ付)	450円
肉入りチャーハン(〃)	600円
五目チャーハン(〃)	600円
カニチャーハン(〃)	700円
中　華　丼	550円
カ ツ 丼	650円
カレーライス	450円

中華 栃 尾

音羽通1丁目新光文社前

(933) 2 5 4 6

① ③ ②

① *Menrui* (left column)
Noodle soup

Ramen Ramen

Wantan Wanton

Omori rāmen Large-size ramen

Tanmen Noodles with clear broth and vegetables

Moyashi soba Noodles with bean sprouts

Ninniku rāmen Garlic ramen

etc.

② *Yaki menrui* (center column, from the middle)
Assorted stir-fried noodles

Yawarakai yakisoba Stir-fried noodles

Katai yakisoba Deep-fried noodles

Niku yakisoba Stir-fried noodles with pork

Gomoku yakisoba "Five-flavored" stir-fried noodles

Gomoku katai yakisoba "Five-flavored" deep-fried noodles

③ *Gohan* (right column)
Rice

Chāhan (sūpu tsuki) Fried rice (with soup)

Nikuiri chāhan (sūpu tsuki) Fried rice with meat (with soup)

Gomoku chāhan (sūpu tsuki) "Five-flavored" stir-fried rice
(with soup)

Kani chāhan (sūpu tsuki) Crab stir-fried rice (with soup)

Chūkadon Stir-fried vegetables and meat over rice.

Katsudon Fried pork over rice.

Karēraise Curry rice

Chūka Tochio
(name of the restaurant)

Part

3

Making Sense of It All

Smoke Gets in Your Eyes, Hair...

As a confirmed non-smoker, I believe that Japan is as slow as a glacier when it comes to considering the rights of non-smokers to breathe fresh air. I can recall going to Nikko about fifteen years ago on the special express train that makes the trip in just one hour and forty-five minutes. My anticipation of the joys of breathing in fresh mountain air at my destination were considerably tempered upon entering a smoke-filled train at Asakusa Station. As is the custom, the smokers among the passengers had lit up the minute they had settled into their seats, and within moments the entire train was redolent with cigarette smoke. Clutching at my throat, I decided to ask the attendant if there was a non-smoking carriage.

"Oh no, sir," he said, smiling eagerly. "Go ahead. You can smoke wherever you want."

These days, most trains include one or two non-smoking carriages. Non-smoking areas have even spread to station platforms, where more and more signs exhort passengers to refrain from lighting up. Unfortunately, this only delays the moment of lighting up until the smokers leave the station precincts. The result is that the walk between station and workplace is now spent dodging clouds of smoke exhaled by nicotine addicts.

According to a survey done by Japan Tobacco in 1992, sixty percent of men and thirteen percent of women in Japan smoke. Interestingly enough, those who do not work said they did not smoke at all or smoke very little while almost seventy percent of all men in their thirties smoke, implying a link between smoking and stress, or at least work.

① 終日禁煙

② 駅構内は終日禁煙です。

ご協力をお願いいたします。

③ 帝都高速度交通営団

① *Shūjistu kin'en*
No smoking all day

② *Eki kōnai wa shūjitsu kin'en desu.*
No smoking in the station premises throughout the day.

Gokyōryoku wo onegai itashimasu.
Your cooperation is requested.

③ *Teito Kōsokudo Kōtsū Eidan*
Teito Rapid Transit Corporation

Toilets

It is 8:30 A.M. and you are on your way to work. While walking through the subway station in Tokyo, your morning's coffee begins to activate your bladder and you feel the need to seek out the nice clean bathroom on the mezzanine floor. You make a beeline for it.

AAAaaargghh!

In the men's toilet stands a diminutive, middle-aged cleaning lady with green rubber gloves on her hands and a mop at the ready. But wait! There is a sign outside the bathroom which says the men's bathroom might be closed, but it's okay to use the women's! Relief.

The range of toilets in Japan is as great as the difference between third-world and first-world standards of living. In some remote train stations and even in private homes, you can still find non-flushing squat toilets. On the other end of the spectrum are exclusive models which lift their lids when users approach and have heated seats, odor exhaust fans, bidets, cleansing water jets, and hot air dryers activated by infrared remote control consoles. The latter type of toilet is the direction the nation is heading towards. Already, more than thirty percent of the toilets in the country now shower, blow-dry, and warm a user's bottom. Top Ten Toilet awards and Toilet Day, December 2nd, help promote this movement. If you think that this obsession with toilets is a recent phenomena you're mistaken. Jun'ichiro Tanizaki (1886–1965), the honored author and literary genius of Japan, devoted long sections of his work, *In Praise of Shadows*, to eulogizing toilets.

SIGNS AT A PUBLIC BATHROOM

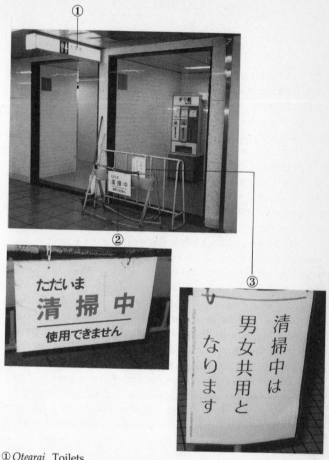

① *Otearai* Toilets

② *Tadaima seisōchū. Shiyō dekimasen.*
Now being cleaned. Cannot be used.

③ *Seisōchū wa danjo kyōyō to narimasu.*
While one bathroom is being cleaned, the other bathroom is for both men and women.

Screech

Know the feeling? A thousand fingernails scraping across a blackboard. Dentists' drills going at full blast. Knuckles being cracked.

I am walking along the sidewalk when suddenly my ears are assailed by yet another bicycle braking to a stop. Knowing that cyclists would probably stand a good chance of being run down if they took to the road is little compensation when you hear the ear-splitting sound of a set of brakes unnervingly close behind you. The sidewalk is a war zone between pedestrians and cyclists. The two were never made to mix, but mix is what they do in most Japanese cities these days.

Hence my paranoia when I'm walking. As a pedestrian, I often have the feeling I am in the timid minority on sidewalks which have been taken over by cyclists weaving in and out and crisscrossing my path with lightning speed and impunity. In Tokyo, the Metropolitan Police Department has certified about half of the city's sidewalks for legal use by cyclists. Signs placed along sidewalks indicate this; however, the signs are superfluous. The police make little effort to enforce the rule that cyclists must dismount and clear the way for pedestrians, or that they must ride on the outside of the sidewalk. Entire generations of cyclists probably know nothing about the regulations, forcing an entire generations of pedestrians into accepting the screeching of brakes that accompanies them down the street.

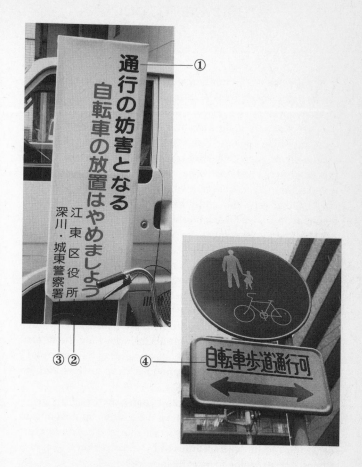

① *Tsūkō no bōgai to naru jitensha no hōchi wa yamemashō.*
Let's not leave our bicycles where they will block the passage.

② *Kōtō Kuyakusho* Koto Ward Office

③ *Fukagawa • Jōtō Keisatsusho* Fukagawa • Joto Police Stations

④ *Jitensha hodō tsukō-ka.* You may ride bicycles on this sidewalk.

Crash, Bang, Boom

When I was first thinking of moving to my present abode in the heart of Tokyo, I carefully reconnoitered the area, assessing its advantages and disadvantages. The first thing that struck me about the place was the din from a nearby factory. After some thought I decided that I could live with this assault on my ears. Only after I moved in did several construction sites go up, just across the canal next to my bedroom. The construction sites have recently become sources of tremendous crashes, drillings, and amplified announcements. All of this begins at around 8:30 each morning.

The energy, expended on producing noise every day in Japan ranges from 18,000 to 30,000 kilowatt-hours. This noise itself is equivalent to 8 million people packed into a one-square-kilometer area, all talking at once.

It feels as if all 8 million are in my neighborhood when a helicopter flies over or the wastepaper collector comes along the street with a friendly blast from his loudspeaker. When this noise is combined with the high-decibel attack by the factory and construction sites, it transcends my level of tolerance and I start fantasizing about green mountains, clear streams, and the distant call of nightingales.

Construction companies are of course aware of the problems they cause, and they duly put up signs apologizing to nearby residents. An apology is a nice thought, but it offers little comfort to those of us afflicted by construction companies all desperately trying to meet their deadlines.

① *Gomeiwaku wo okakeshite makotoni sumimasen.*
We are truly sorry for causing any disturbances.

② *Anzen, sōon niwa toku ni ki wo tsukete sagyō shite orimasu kara shibaraku no aida gokyōryoku wo onegai shimasu.*
We are paying attention to safety and noise while working, and we ask for your patience for a while.

Stickers for Luck

Next time you visit a Shinto shrine, check for small stickers bearing names affixed to the main gateway and other parts of the shrine. You might find the name of someone famous. If it is your local shrine, chances are you'll find the name of your friendly butcher, tofu vendor, or real estate agent. Those stickers are *senja-fuda*, which means "thousand shrine labels."

The custom of pasting labels of one's name on shrine entrances dates back centuries. As the word suggests, people who embarked on a pilgrimage to visit as many shrines as possible would have name labels specially made so that they could leave their own record of attendance at each shrine and, presumably, accrue plenty of favor with the gods along the way.

Another type of *fuda* shown here is a *yaku-yoke-fuda*, a misfortune-avoiding label, in other words, a talisman. When I had to go into the hospital for an operation, I was instructed to keep one near my hospital bed which read "expel sickness." But unlike the usual word for sickness which combines the Chinese characters for "disease" and "spirit," this one was composed of "disease" and "demon."

Senja-fuda were traditionally hand-printed with a wooden block on Japanese paper. More modern printing methods are now used. You can get your own name printed on custommade *senja-fuda* at almost any small printing service. Its design, the number of colors used, and its size all determine the ultimate cost. About three hundred *senja-fuda* measuring two-and-a-half centimeters by seven centimeters in two basic colors will cost about 30,000 yen.

LUCKY STICKERS

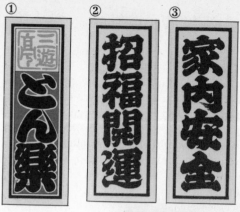

Pillar at a shrine

① *San'yūtei Tonraku*　(Name of a *rakugo* performer)

② *Shōfuku kaiun*
Bring in happiness and open the doors to good fortune.

③ *Kanai anzen*　Keep the family safe.

Wanted

Has anybody seen Goto Eiji? The police want him for the shootings of two leaders of the Yamaguchi-gumi, Japan's largest gang, in Osaka in 1985. Goto is missing the ends of his right- and left-hand pinky fingers. He has tattoos of carp on his right arm, a carp, samurai, and cherry blossoms on his left arm, and more cherry blossoms and dragons on his back, extending below his buttocks.

Goto's victims were part of a *bōryokudan*, violent gang, the police term for *yakuza*. These gangs rarely pose a direct threat to the public except on the rare occasions when their own internal struggles or territorial disputes spill over into street shootings. Their most common crimes, in order of frequency, are violation of the Drug Control Law, infliction of bodily injury, gambling, blackmail, larceny, and bookmaking.

In 1992, a new anti-gang law came into effect. Under the law, organizations with a certain number of members with criminal records are designated "underworld organizations," which allows police to crack down on them if they engage in specified criminal activities, including collecting protection fees from businesses, demanding unreasonable loans or demanding monetary contributions under various pretenses, and forcing loans to be repaid at illegally high interest rates. As of December 1992, sixteen gangs, including the three largest—Yamaguchi-gumi, Inagawakai, and Sumiyoshikai—were designated under the Anti-gang Law.

If you happen to know Goto's whereabouts, or if you need police assistance, dial 110 or go to any one of the closest *kōban*, or police boxes.

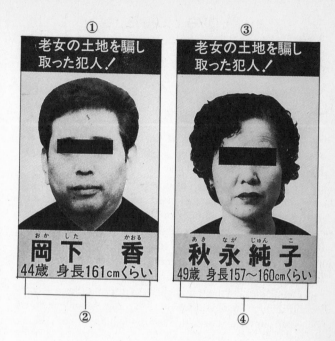

① *Rōjo no tochi wo damashitotta hannin!*
A criminal who deceived an elderly woman and stole her land!

② *Okashita Kaoru* (Name of the man)

 44 sai, Shinchō 161cm kurai
 44 years-old, Height about 161 cm

③ *Rōjo no tochi wo damashitotta hannin!*
A criminal who deceived an elderly woman and stole their land!

④ *Akinaga Junko* (Name of the woman)

 49 sai, Shinchō 157–160cm kurai
 49 years-old, Height about 157–160 cm

Love Hotels

Chandeliers, revolving beds, transparent bathtubs over-flowing with bubbles, rooms decorated with a Las Vegas or sumptuous European palace theme—these elements to inspire romance and excitement can be found in love hotels. Love hotels, as the name implies, cater to couples wishing to have a private venue for their trysts. Standard love hotels ensure the anonymity of their customers by removing all face-to-face contact between the customers and staff. If you visit by car, the parking lot is underground or cars are hidden from prying eyes by a high wall or maybe even curtains to cover the car's license plates. Instead of a front check-in counter staffed with very visible people, customers can select a room of their choice by viewing a video or an illuminated display of the rooms available. Payment and check-out formalities are completed through a small window in each room. Some love hotels even space out the exit of customers in the hallways or parking lot.

Older generations of love hotels built between the 1960s and 1980s usually advertise their presence with bright neon lights, fake castle turrets, or even copies of the Statue of Liberty on their roofs. In recent years, they have attempted to tone down their appearances, and it has become more difficult to spot the difference between a love hotel and a business hotel. But only love hotels offer a two- to three- hour "rest" rate that ranges from 1,200 to 12,600 yen and an overnight 10 P.M. to 10 A.M. "stay" rate that is about twenty percent higher. And once inside, sleekly designed rooms with wall-to-wall mirrors, the selection of videos, and courtesy condoms will betray the love hotel's true nature.

SIGN AT ENTRANCE OF A LOVE HOTEL

Love hotel

① *Rāku* Lark (name of the hotel)

② *Kyūkei…3,900 yen* Rest…3,900 yen
 Shukuhaku…5,900 yen Overnight stay…5,900 yen
 Kin'itsu Set rate

③ *Taimu-sābisu ari (do • nichi nozoku)*
 Discount times available (not including Sat. • Sun.)

Hanko

Though you can get by in Japan without a personal seal these days, much bother can be avoided by purchasing one. In Japan, personal seals are known as *hanko* or *inkan*. I finally bought myself one when I wanted to invest some money with a securities company. I knew the securities company would insist I had one. It is the one way the government has of insuring that gangsters do not launder their money through the securities companies. Although a *hanko* usually uses your surname, this need not be the case. I chose two Chinese characters which correspond to the sound of my first name for my *hanko*. Since I settled for a wooden one, it cost barely more than a thousand yen.

When receiving an express delivery parcel, filling out your tax return, opening a bank account or even when investing in a securities company—in all these cases, I have been able to use my *hanko* as a *mitomein*, an unregistered seal. However, it is recommended that everyone have a *jitsuin*, a registered seal for important documents like housing contracts or notarized deeds. In effect, registering a seal means that the seal's shape, right down to its tiniest imperfections, is recorded as being yours alone, much like a human fingerprint. Only one *jitsuin* is allowed per person and this *jitsuin* is for that person's use alone. Please note that although a *jitsuin* may be made of wood, ivory, or stone, ward and town offices refuse to register a seal which does not include a surname or have a border around it.

For very important contracts, the other party may insist on proof that the seal affixed to the document is actually your *jitsuin*. In such instances, the town or local ward office where you registered the seal will supply you with an *inkan shōmeisho*, or a proof-of-seal document.

① Tamaru Tamiya Tamura Tayama Taga Tada Date Taira Daigo Daichi Daimon

② Takagi Takagi Takaku Takakura Takasu Takasugi Takakuwa Takasaki Takazawa Takase Takada

③ Takahashi Takahata Takahata Takahama Takabayashi Takahara Takamatsu Takami Takamizawa Takamiya Takamura

④ Takarada Takano Taki Takigawa Takiguchi Takizawa Takino Takimoto Takei Takeuchi Takeoka

⑤ Taketani Takenaka Takeuouchi Takeno Takebayashi Takehara Takemura Takemoto Takemori Takeyama Takei

⑥ Takebe Takemura Takemoto Takeyama Tachibana Tateishi Tatekawa Tateno Tachibana Tatsumi Tatsumi

Cram Schools

I always find it hard to imagine what it must be like to be a child in junior high school dividing my days between home, school, and *juku*, or cram school. When I try to recollect my own school days, I can recall nothing but long days of sheer boredom at school, tempered by other days spent camping in the country or swimming at nearby beaches, always activities shared with friends. However, that was in Australia, where Confucianism doesn't rule the educational system and nature is readily accessible from even the major cities.

The really hard grind for children in Japan often begins in the second and third years of junior high, when students begin to feel the pressure to enter the right high school, the first essential step to gaining entry to the desired university, which helps them enter a desired company. This pressure drives students in droves to the nation's *juku*. They flock there each day after school hours to put in yet more hours, frequently going over subject matter a year more advanced than the Education Ministry's curriculum considers appropriate for their age. Parents of junior high school children part with an average monthly fee of about 18,000 yen for sending junior high students to *juku*, a sum which is roughly double the cost of sending a child to a normal public school. That *juku* tuition fee does not include the cost of admission, books, exams, or transportation.

About half of all Japanese children get additional hours of eduction outside of normal school hours. When figures are narrowed to just those of junior high school age, eighty percent get extra instruction and sixty-six percent go to *juku*. So great is the pressure to succeed via the *juku* that this two-tiered educational system has been replicated overseas wherever Japanese gather in substantial numbers.

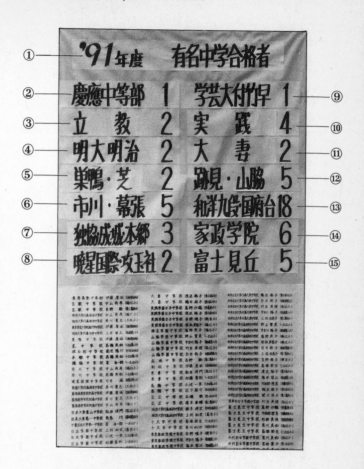

① *91 nendo yūmei chūgaku gōkakusha*
Successful entrants to famed junior high schools
in the '91 [academic] year.

② *Keiō Chūtōbu*
Keio Junior High

③ *Rikkyō*
Rikkyo

④ *Meidai Meiji*
Meiji University [Junior High]

⑤ *Sugamo • Shiba*
Sugamo • Shiba

⑥ *Ichikawa • Makuhari*
Ichikawa • Makuhari

⑦ *Dokkyō • Seijō • Hongō*
Dokkyo • Seijo • Hongo

⑧ *Gyōseikokusai • Kōgyokusha*
Gyōsei International • Kōgyokusha

⑨ *Gakugeidai Fu[zoku] Takehaya*
Tokyo Gakugei University [Junior High], Takehaya branch

⑩ *Jissen*
Jissen

⑪ *Ōtsuma*
Otsuma Junior High

⑫ *Atomi • Yamawaki*
Atomi • Yamawaki

⑬ *Wayō Kudan • Kōnodai*
Wayo Kudan • Wayo Konodai

⑭ *Kasei Gakuin*
Kasei Gakuin

⑮ *Fujimigaoka*
Fujimigaoka

Students celebrating their acceptance
into Tokyo University

Part

4

Helpful Perks

Libraries

Libraries, *toshokan*, are fairly liberally scattered about Japan. Though they mainly cater to the Japanese-language reader, you may discover that your local library is quite a useful resource. Many libraries in areas with large non-Japanese populations keep foreigners' needs in mind. Libraries in such areas often have a collection of foreign language materials, including books, newspapers, and magazines. Even in areas with few foreign residents, many libraries have English-language newspapers and magazines for Japanese readers. These include The Japan Times, The Asian Wall Street Journal, The International Herald-Tribune, and the Asian editions of Newsweek and Time.

In major cities like Tokyo, Osaka, and Nagoya, many wards have a central library which stocks multiple copies for lending out to branch libraries. Interlibrary loans can take up to three weeks to process. Recently, libraries have begun purchasing CDs, videos, and records. Though many libraries have a large number of audiotapes, currently they are only available to the visually impaired. Due to the large number of inquiries, many libraries are considering making these available to the general public. If so, they would provide a great resource material for learning Japanese.

To receive a library card, bring your alien registration card or driver's license to your local library. You can use any library in the prefecture from which your library card was issued; if you like, you can get cards from more than one prefecture. Though hours vary from one library to another, most are open from about nine in the morning until about six in the evening from Tuesday to Sunday.

CAR RENTAL COMPANY'S SIGNBOARD

A freeway in Tokyo

① *Nissan Rentakā*
  Nissan Rent-A-Car

② *Kā rīsu*
  Car lease

The Handyman Can

Most people don't keep frogs, so most people don't have a frog problem. But a man I know had too many frogs. They couldn't resist the pond he had in his back garden. That was the year there was a bumper rainy season, and conditions were ripe for frogs to breed and multiply.

The man was fond of frogs as long as there were only a small number in his pond croaking away to remind him of that Basho haiku about the frog jumping into the pond, making its little existential splash—nature's reminder of the silence that comes before and after. However, the sudden frog population explosion that particular year bothered him. The frog chorus croaked night and day. Neither he nor the neighbors could sleep.

So he rang a *benriya*, a handyman. The *benriya* responded to the man's call with bags which he filled with errant frogs. He took the frogs to a new home, a pond in a public park.

My own experience with a *benriya* grew out of an offer of furniture from a friend. I had spent my last yen on a new apartment, had no money left for furniture, and was using a cardboard box for a kitchen table and a pile of dictionaries for a chair, when a friend offered me some of her mother's furniture that was being stored in a warehouse. To carry me and the furniture back to the apartment, I simply hired the services of a *benriya*. The phone book lists plenty of *benriya*.

Want your roof drains cleared of leaves? Need someone to babysit your bedridden grandmother while you do the shopping? Has your garden become overgrown while you were overseas? Are you fed up with the pigeons on your roof? Do you need the tiles in your bathroom replaced?

Call a *benriya*.

ADVERTISEMENT FOR A HANDYMAN
ON A BENCH AT A BUS STOP

① *Hōmū Sābisu Sentā* Home Service Center

② *Benriya* Handyman

③ *Toshima-ku Nagasaki 4-33-17* (Address of handyman)

④ *Hikkoshi, Mitsumori muryō* Moving, Free estimate

⑤ *Daiku-kōji, Kurosu-kōji* Carpentry, Wallpaper repairs
  Suidō-kōji, Tairu-kōji Plumbing, Tiling
  Penki-tosō, Ashiba Painting, Scaffolding
  Toyo-shūri, Amamori Gutter repair, Roof leak
  Niwa-shigoto, Sōji Garden work, Cleaning
  Sodai-gomi, Gomi-shobun Collection of large garbage and trash

A Drink, a Snack, and a Friend

For anyone wanting a drink, a meal, and a bit of company after a hard day's work in the office, head to an *izakaya*. *Izakaya* are the Japanese equivalent of the pubs or small taverns in England or America. You can usually spot an *izakaya* by its red lantern, or *akachōchin*, hung outside; *akachōchin* is also another name for an *izakaya*.

During the immediate postwar years in Japan, when most of the population had little money, *izakaya* spread as cheap friendly places to get drinks and snacks. *Izakaya* serve simple dishes from three hundred to six hundred yen a plate. Beer, sake, and *shōchū* are the standard drinks.

Friends meeting for a night on the town at an *izakaya* can fill their stomachs and have a few drinks for a reasonable tab of around 3,000 yen apiece. This price is attractive, specially compared to hostess bars, snack bars, or *snakku*, and bars, which charge high overheads for a few peanuts and a shot of whisky from a bottle that you have already purchased.

One of my favorite *akachōchin* is in Shibuya. With seating for only seven to eight people and a waitress serving hot sake, the atmosphere is convivial and family-like. As those who frequent *izakaya* can attest, an *izakaya* is a place where customers let their guards down and talk to the people sitting next to them. Perhaps for this reason, *izakaya* are regarded as good places to go for *nijikai*, follow-up parties, after more formal celebrations. Who knows, drop by your local *akachochin* and maybe the man who stands in line with you for the train everyday may feel uninhibited enough to start chatting with you.

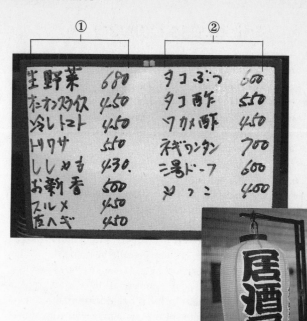

Akachōchin

① *Nama yasai* Fresh vegetables
   Onion Suraisu Sliced Onions
   Hiyashi Tomato Chilled tomatoes
   Toriwasa Boiled chicken with horseradish
   Shishamo Grilled baby fish
   Oshinkō Pickles
   Surume Broiled dried squid
   Kawahagi Grilled fish
② *Takobutsu* Octopus sashimi
   Takozu Vinegared Octopus
   Wakamezu Vinegared seaweed
   Negi wantan Pork wanton soup with scallions
   Yudōfu Boiled tofu
   Yakko Chilled tofu

Express Delivery

A number of companies which promise to get items to their destination as quickly as possible rival the post office in the fast delivery business in Japan. They deal with *takuhai-bin*, or express mail delivery. These companies deliver everything from letters to ice cream to luggage.

When I left my sunglasses at a friend's house during a visit to Kyushu, the friend sent them to Tokyo for me, using an express delivery service. Two days later, they arrived perfectly intact. I wasn't home on the day they were delivered and found a notice in my mailbox giving the telephone number of the closest branch of a delivery company. I rang and arranged for delivery at a time when I knew I would be home.

Golfers and skiiers also make good use of delivery services. Skis or golf clubs can be sent a couple of days in advance to avoid having to carry them to the office during rush hour on the day you're to leave. Most of the companies will get your set of golf clubs or skis to your destination within one or two days for just under 1,500 yen.

The five biggest express delivery companies in Japan are Yamato, Sagawa Kyubin, Nittsu, Fukuyama Tsuun, and Seino Unyu. Each company charges according to different criteria. For example, Yamato charges by a combination of weight and the total length, width, and height of your parcel, with a maximum of twenty kilograms or 120 centimeters, while Sagawa Kyubin calculates according to weight.

Companies have branches in the most unexpected places. The small family-run photo and printing service in my neighborhood doubles as an agency for two of the express delivery companies. Since most the neighborhood get their photos printed there, and the store is more conveniently located than the post office, everyone knows to bring in their parcels when they want items express delivered.

①

②

③

① *Kuroneko Yamato no Takkyūbin*
Black Cat Yamato Express
delivery (this expression is a
Yamato Transportation trademark)

② *Nittsū no Perikan-bin*
Nippon Express Pelican
Courier

Nippon zenkoku doa kara doa e
Door-to-door delivery nation-
wide

Hikkoshi mo dōzo
Home removal service also
available

Nippon Tsūun
Nippon Express

③ *Te kara te e ai no messenjā*
Delivered from hand-to-hand
with love

Futtowāku
Footwork

Takuhai, konimotsu toritsugiten
Drop-off center for home-
delivery and small package
delivery

Neighborhood Activities

For anyone with even a smattering of Japanese, one golden opportunity to actually become a part of the community is to join your local *chōnaikai*, the neighborhood association. *Chōnaikai* began before World War II as quasi-government organizations with up to one hundred households in one association which coordinated local activities. During the war, they were used to rally support for the wartime cause and as a subtle means of thought control. Abolished by the Occupation forces in the immediate postwar years, they were partially restored in the 1950s and now exist as nominally independent and voluntary organizations.

The membership fee for a *chōnaikai* is minimal. Households in my *chōnaikai* contribute 3,600 yen annually. In return, members regularly receive a newsletter and can participate in various events.

Some of the mail in your mailbox might even come from the *chōnaikai*—announcements about festivals, meetings of the *chōnaikai*, events for Respect for the Aged Day in September, a fund-raising bazaar, or notification of the venue and time for a local fire drill. *Chōnaikai* also help organize the spring and autumn national road safety campaigns, parent and children gatherings, and block parties in the summer. Most *chōnaikai* also have youth and women auxiliaries.

To join, please ask your neighbors who the head of your *chōnaikai* is. Be an ambassador for your country, get all the neighborhood gossip, and make friends at the same time.

TYPICAL *CHŌNAIKAI* ANNOUNCEMENT

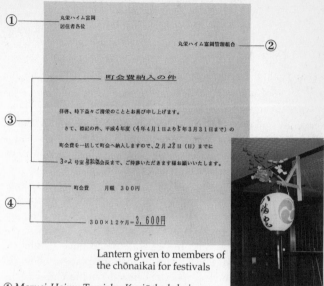

丸栄ハイム富岡
居住者各位

丸栄ハイム富岡管理組合 — ②

町会費納入の件

拝啓、時下益々ご清栄のこととお喜び申し上げます。

さて、標記の件、平成4年度（4年4月1日より5年3月31日まで）の

町会費を一括して町会へ納入しますので、2月28日（日）までに

3o2号室 村松副会長まで、ご持参いただきます様お願いいたします。

町会費 月額 300円

300×12ケ月＝3,600円

Lantern given to members of
the chōnaikai for festivals

① *Maruei-Haimu Tomioka, Kyojūsha kakui*
To all those who live in the Maruei-Haimu Tomioka complex

② *Maruei-Haimu Tomioka Kanri-kumiai*
The management association of Maruei-Haimu Tomioka

③ *Chōkaihi nōnyū no ken: haikei, jika masumasu goseiei no koto to
oyorokobi mōshiagemasu. Sate, hyōki no ken, Heisei 4 nendo (4 nen 4
gatsu 1 nichi yori 3 gatsu 31 nichi made) no chōkaihi wo ikkatsu shite
chōkai e nōnyū shimasu node, 2 gatsu 28 nichi (Nichi) made ni 302
gōshitsu Muramatsu Fukukaichō made gojisan itadakimasuyō onegai
itashimasu.*
Regarding the block association fee: In this season, we trust that
everyone is well and prospering. With regards to the matter
above, since we will bring the block association fees for the fiscal
year of Heisei 4 (from Heisei 4 April 1 till Heisei 5 March 31) to
the block association all at once, we ask that everyone bring their
money to Vice President Muramatsu in apartment #302 by February 28 (Sun.).

④ *Chōkaihi getsugaku: 300 yen*
Block association fee per month: 300 yen

300x12 kagetsu=3,600 yen   300x12 months=3,600 yen

Orders of the Bath

When I first moved into my present apartment, I was stuck without hot water for a few days, so I visited the nearby *sentō*, bathhouse. It turned out to be a pleasant experience. Even those with baths at home still occasionally visit the local bathhouse just to sample the atmosphere and the hedonistic pleasure of soaking in the more spacious surroundings provided by such establishments.

In Japan, visiting the bathhouse is a time-honored tradition dating from a time when most of the population commuted daily to the bath, in part to keep clean, and in part to catch up on neighborhood gossip. Unlike in the old days, however, the sexes are now separated by separate bathrooms. Bathhouse operators with any sense of pride keep the place spotless. In many cases, bathhouse operators install bubble baths, baths with various herbal medicines, drink machines, or sauna rooms to attract more customers.

There are, however, certain rules and requirements to be observed, since a *sentō* may sometimes be visited by several hundred locals in one evening. The rules are mostly common sense. As with any Japanese bath, you don't wash in the bath. Lather up, scrub down, and rinse off before getting in the bath. Then get in and soak. Many bathhouses rule that no customers with tattoos covering their bodies may use the bath. This regulation is an attempt to screen out *yakuza*, the Japanese mafia, who are known for their love of tattoos.

お客様にお願い

① お互いに気分よくご入浴できるよう次の事にご協力下さい

(1)浴槽に入る前に身体を洗い流しましょう

(2)浴槽内でタオルを使わないで下さい

(3)湯水の出し放しは止めましょう

(4)カランは必ず手で押しましょう

(5)他の人に湯水がかからないようにしましょう

(6)濡れた身体で脱衣場に入らないで下さい

(7)お年寄りと幼児には付添いを付けて下さい

(8)酒に酔ってのご入浴はお断り致します

(9)伝染病・皮膚病の方はお断り致します

(10)ロッカー・下駄箱の〝かぎ〟は持ち帰らないで下さい

東京都公衆浴場業環境衛生同業組合

浴　場　主

Public bath house

① *Okyakusama ni onegai.*
Requests we would like to ask of the customers.

② *Otagai ni kibunyoku gonyūyoku dekiru yō tsugi no koto ni gokyōryoku kudasai.*
In order that you may bathe comfortably, please observe the following rules.

91

③ 1. *Yokusō ni hairu mae ni karada wo arainagashimashō.*
Before entering the bath tub, please wash and rinse yourself off.

④ 2. *Yokusō-nai de taoru wo tsukawanaide kudasai.*
Please do not use your washcloth in the bath.

⑤ 3. *Yumizu no dashippanashi wa yamemashō.*
Please do not leave the water running.

⑥ 4. *Karan wa kanarazu te de oshimashō.*
Always push the faucet with your hands.

⑦ 5. *Hoka no hito ni yumizu ga kakaranai yōni shimashō.*
Please make sure the water you're using doesn't splash on anyone else.

⑧ 6. *Nureta karada de datsuijō ni hairanaide kudasai.*
Please dry off before entering the changing room.

⑨ 7. *Otoshiyori to yōji niwa tsukisoi wo tsukete kudasai.*
Please be sure to accompany elderly persons and children.

⑩ 8. *Sake ni yotte no gonyūyoku wa okotowari itashimasu.*
Bathing under the influence of alcohol is not permitted.

⑪ 9. *Densenbyō, hifubyō no kata wa okotowari itashimasu.*
Persons with infectious diseases or skin diseases are not permitted.

⑫ 10. *Rokkā, getabako no kagi wa mochikaeranaide kudasai.*
Please do not take locker or shoe locker key home.

⑬ *Tōkyō-to Kōshū Yokujōgyō Kankyō-eisei Dōgyō-kumiai*
Tokyo Metropolitan Public Bath House Environmental Hygiene Trade Association.

Yokujō nushi
The owner

Leisure

Taking a Break

Japan has as many public holidays as most other advanced industrialized nations. So why do statistics show everyone works long hours? Overtime work and short paid leave.

January 1—*Ganjistu*, New Year's Day: A day for offering prayers at shrines or temples and greeting friends.

January 15—*Seijin no Hi*, Coming of Age Day: Twenty-year-olds dress in kimono or suits to attend ceremonies marking their entrance into adulthood.

February 11—*Kenkoku Kinen no Hi*, National Founding Day: The first emperor of Japan established his capital in the Yamato district near present day Nara.

Around March 20th—*Shunbun no Hi*, Spring Equinox: A time to clean the graves of ancestors.

Around April 29 to May 5—*Gōruden Uīku*, Golden Week: A week with consecutive holidays. Holidays include: *Midori no Hi*, Green Day: April 29; *Kenpō Kinenbi*, Constitution Day: May 3; a national holiday: May 4; and *Kodomo no Hi*, Children's Day: May 5.

September 15—*Keirō no Hi*, Respect for the Aged Day: The media announces the oldest person in Japan. Senior citizens give their secrets to longevity.

September 23—see opposite page.

October 10—*Taiiku no Hi*, Sports Day: Commemorates the Tokyo Olympic Games in 1964 with school athletic meetings.

November 3—*Bunka no Hi*, Culture Day: The government gives citations to persons of cultural or scientific merit.

November 23—*Kinrō Kansha no Hi*, Labor Thanksgiving Day: Lie around the house and dream about a day with no overtime.

December 23—*Tennō Tanjōbi*, Emperor's Birthday: The birthday of Emperor Akihito. Visit the Imperial Palace and yell "Banzai."

① *1993 9 gatsu Heisei 5 nen* 1993 September Heisei 5

② *Shūbun no hi, Mokuyō, Higan no chūnichi*
Equinox Day, Thursday, The peak of Equinox week
[Buddhist services are performed during this week]

Shūbun Equinox

③ *Shō, 9 gatsu 23 nichi, Kyū: 8 gatsu 8 ka*
Thirty-day month, September 23, According
to the lunar calendar: August 8

Hinoto hitsuji, Goō • Senbu
According to an old Chinese calendar: Sheep, According
to a different old Chinese calendar: Bad Luck Day

④ *Shigoto wo suru toki wa jōkigen de yare.*
When working, work cheerfully.

95

Ryokan and Pensions

Getting away from it all can be a real pleasure in Japan, if you choose a time when the rest of the nation isn't doing the same. For those of us working in an urban environment, a trip to the countryside reminds us of Japan's majestic landscape. Holidays spent deep in the mountains or by the sea are especially rewarding if you choose to stay at traditional Japanese inns known as *ryokan*.

At a *ryokan*, you will receive the undivided attention of the staff from the moment you enter. Your shoes will be taken and you will receive a pair of slippers to use. Sumptuous meals will be served in your traditional-style tatami room. Your futon will be laid out for you. Finally, every *ryokan* offers patrons the greatest of Japanese indulgences, a bath. Most *ryokan* have stone or wooden baths the size of small pools. My favorite *ryokan* overlooks a running stream in a small valley. In autumn, crickets sit on the window sill and serenade the bathers. All the pampering you receive at a *ryokan* does add up—some charge 30,000 yen a night.

For those who can't afford such luxuries, pensions and *minshuku* are a cheaper alternative. Most are private homes with boarding facilities. You lay out your own futon. Dinners and lunches are sometimes not available. The bath is basic and hours for bathing are more limited. Despite these drawbacks, *minshuku* and pensions can be a delightful way to stay in beautiful locations and meet other travelers.

Finally, a number of inns offer discounts to residents of certain wards or towns. Some wards have their own *ryokan*. As a resident, you are entitled to use these facilities. The only stipulation is that you book through the ward or town office and take your chances with a waiting list if you choose a popular time.

SIGN AT A *RYOKAN*

—①

A traditional-style
Japanese *minshuku*

① *Ryokan Hōmeikan*
 Homeikan Inn

Sake

In a story among the classic repertoire of *rakugoka*, comic story-tellers, a father and son both vow to give up drinking sake. Soon after making their vow, the son visits a customer who tempts him with a drink of sake to celebrate the arrival of spring. The son refuses, angering the customer, who retorts that he will take his business elsewhere. Upon hearing this, the son says he doesn't care if he loses the customer, ada- mantly insisting that he must keep his promise. The customer praises the son for being man enough to keep his promise and sug- gests they drink to it. The son agrees and together they down two large bottles of sake and get nicely drunk.

As the story exemplifies, in Japan you'll drink for any occa- sion and reason: weddings, funerals, festivals, New Year's, farewell parties. Sake is the nation's alcoholic beverage. Made from rice, sake came to Japan not long after the introduction of wet rice cultivation in 300 B.C. Since then, the pleasures of drinking sake have transcended the boundaries of Japan. Peo- ple in New York, London, and Bangkok enjoy sake.

According to experts, a good sake has a mellow fragrance and a blend of five flavors: sweetness, sourness, pungency, bit- terness, and astringency. The grade of sake—Second Class, First Class, and Special Class—was once a reliable guide to quality. But since higher taxes are attached to higher grades, many brands ceased submitting their sake for grading. As a rule, the best sake comes from Nada near Kobe, Fushimi near Kyoto, and Akita and Hiroshima prefectures. All areas boast good rice-growing conditions and pure water.

SAKE BARRELS

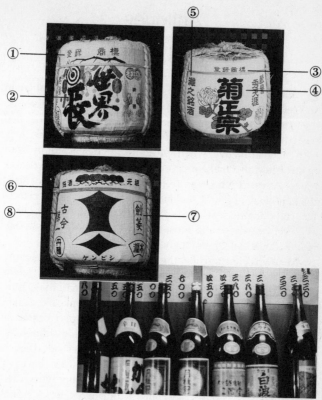

Sake bottles

① *Tōroku shōhyō*
Registered trademark

② *Sekaichō*
(Brand name of sake)

③ *Tōroku shōhyō*
Registered trademark

④ *Kikumasamune*
(Brand name of sake)

⑤ *Nada no meishu*
Nada local speciality

⑥ *Meishu ganso*
Maker of choice sake

⑦ *Kenbishi*
(Brand name of sake)

⑧ *Kokon-daichi*
Finest sake since the beginning of
time

Antiques

Some of the most beautiful and unusual keepsakes of Japan can be found with a bit of effort and rummaging through the boxes of knickknacks at flea markets. Such items, rescued from the dust-laden obscurity of country farmhouses, look extremely attractive when prominently displayed in your home. They also make marvellous souvenirs for friends back home. A friend who is a do-it-herself interior decorator used the kimono obi I found at a flea market in Kyoto as a spectacular wall hanging just inside the main entrance to her home. With this purchase and most others, I have been able to bargain with the stall operator and bring down the price.

My own collection of antiques were mostly found at temple flea markets and antique markets. In Tokyo, the huge Heiwajima market is held five times a year—in March, May, June, September, and December. At each market, some 250 dealers from all over Japan converge in the huge display center for three days to sell their wares. Their items include old military medals and hats, obsolete carpenters' tools, chests-of-drawers rescued from oblivion in mountain farmhouses, beautiful antique dolls, second-hand kimono and obi, tiny ivory carvings known as *netsuke*, old coins, fading wood-block prints, blue and white porcelain, and lots more.

Japan has about 300,000 licensed antique dealers. That figure might convey the impression that there are endless supplies of antiques in the country. But frequent fires, past civil wars, and World War II were responsible for the loss of many items. So even many legitimate dealers are forced to include merely old things among their genuine antiques. Beware, objects might have the patina of age but may have been made only yesterday.

ADVERTISEMENT FOR ANTIQUE MARKET

A flea market at Tomioka Hachiman Shrine

① *Dai 1 kai Akishima Kottō • Antiiku Feā*
The first Akishima Antique • Curio Fair

② *Seiyō antīku komingu kottō 30 ten*
30 stores selling Western antiques and old handicrafts

③ *JR Akishima-eki, Gesha toho 1 pun*
JR Akishima Station, One minute walk

Mori Taun Hōru   Mori Town Hall

Mori Taun Hobii Kurafutokan   Mori Town Hobby Craft House

Dai-chūshajō ari (yūryō)   Large parking lot available (fee charged)

Nyūjō muryō   Free admission for the fair

④ *Heisei 5 nen 4 gatsu 24 (do) 25 (nichi)*
Heisei 5 April 24th (Sat.) 25th (Sun.)

Renting Videos

Feel like renting a video for a good night's entertainment curled up in the futon with a bagful of popcorn? Before you visit the video rental store, consider the following.

Do you know the Japanese names of the movies you want to see? As a rule, most foreign-language movies, particularly English-language ones, retain something like the original sound of the title. *Mad Max* is *Maddo Makksu*. And *Casablanca* is *Kasaburanka*. But there are exceptions, for instance, *Paris is Burning* is known in Japan as *Paris, Yoru wa Nemurenai*, which translates as *Paris, You Can't Sleep at Night*. Or try asking for *Shadows and Fog*, one of Woody Allen's latest offerings. In this case, the title is a literal rendering of the original, *Kage to Kiri*. But you've got to be in the know to rent *Diary of a Hitman*, which has the title *Sabi Tsuita Jūdan*, or Rusty Bullet.

Would-be renters should be warned to check the fine print on the cover of the video. In some cases you can rent the video about how the movie was made, so you have to take a close look at the title. Other versions do without subtitles and substitute the original soundtrack with a Japanese soundtrack. This is particularly the case with children's animated cartoons. Videos with only a Japanese soundtrack are called *nihongo ban*.

One sure way to find the Japanese language titles for the latest videos is to get the monthly magazine *Video Insider Japan*, published by Gyaga Communications Inc. The magazine, a specialized publication designed for video shop owners and other people in the industry, is not available at stores. For those who would like to have a copy, yearly subscriptions are available through Gyaga Communications at (03) 5410-3504.

AT A VIDEO RENTAL STORE

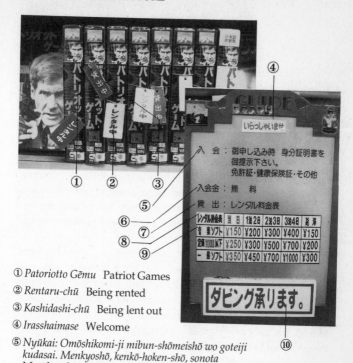

① *Patoriotto Gēmu* Patriot Games

② *Rentaru-chū* Being rented

③ *Kashidashi-chū* Being lent out

④ *Irasshaimase* Welcome

⑤ *Nyūkai: Omōshikomi-ji mibun-shōmeishō wo goteiji kudasai. Menkyoshō, kenkō-hoken-shō, sonota*
Membership: When applying, please bring along an identification card. A driver's license, health insurance card, or other form of identification

⑥ *Nyūkaikin: muryō* Membership fee: free

⑦ *Kashidashi: rentaru ryōkin-hyō*
Rentals: rental price list

⑧ *Rentaru ryōkin-hyō: tōjitsu, 1 paku 2 ka, 2 haku 3 ka, 3 paku 4 ka, entai*
Rental price list: same day, 1 night 2 days, 2 nights 3 days, 3 nights 4 days, late

⑨ *Ongaku sofuto* Music ware

Teika 1,000 ika Items worth less than ¥1,000

Ippan sofuto Regular ware

⑩ *Dabingu uketamawarimasu.* We will also dub videos.

Massage

For centuries, massage was considered a vital part of a person's medical treatment. Masseuse and masseurs were credited with being able to cure all kinds of maladies. An eighth century document states that masseuses and masseurs were part of the Medical Bureau of the government. Then, as now, the masseuse and masseur was known as an *amma-san*. During the seventeenth century, blind *amma-san* were common. The more highly developed sense of touch in a blind person was considered a worthy asset in a person whose selling point lay in an ability to feel out and loosen stiff bone joints and tense muscles.

Amma-san no longer make their presence known by whistling while wandering the streets. But some *amma-san* advertise their services through the mail. And you are probably no more than a phone call and thirty minutes away from the nearest neighborhood *amma-san*, who will readily answer your call and in no time start cracking your joints and alternatively kneading and pummeling you into nirvana.

Another person who may release all the tension in your shoulders is a *shiatsu* therapist. Unlike an *amma-san*, a *shiatsu* therapist places pressure on specific points on the body that are believed to stimulate one's *ki*, or life force. Some people swear by *shiatsu* when it comes to stress-induced stiffness in the body.

Other, more dubious alternatives to the legitimate *amma-san* and *shiatsu* therapists also advertise as masseuses. These masseuses use trade names such as "Wink," "Banana," or "Blue Night" and advertise "fashion massages" and "soft massages" via stickers often found on the insides of telephone booths or in your mailbox. The stickers usually display alluring illustrations of nubile females whose massage talents are questionable.

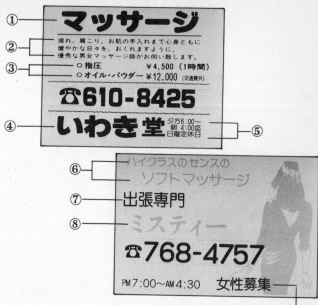

① *Massāji* Massage

② *Tsukare, katakori, ohada no teire made shinshin tomoni sukoyakana hibi wo okuremasu yōni yūshū na danjo massāji-shi ga oukagai itashimasu.*
Relieves fatigue, stiff shoulders, and helps skin care, so your can spend you days in the best of mental and physical health. Excellent male and female masseurs available.

③ *Shiatsu: ¥4,500 (1 jikan)*
Shiatsu: ¥4,500 (one hour)

Oiru, paudā: ¥12,000 (kōtsūhitomo)
Oil massage, powder: ¥12,000 (cost of transport included)

④ *Iwaki-dō*
(Name of the company)

⑤ *Yūgata 6:00 - asa 4:00 made*
6:00 in the evening - till 4:00 in the morning

Nichiyō teikyūbi
Closed on Sunday

⑥ *Hai-kurasu no sensu no sofuto massāji*
Soft massage with a high-class touch

⑦ *Shutchō senmon*
Visiting service only

⑧ *Misutii*
Misty (name of company)

⑨ *Josei boshū* Hiring women

Horse Racing

On any given day in Japan, there can be as many as twelve different tracks holding horse races. Betting on them is simple if you know the ropes. Japan has twenty-two licensed off-track betting centers for horse racing. All you need to do is buy a sports or horse racing newspaper and a betting card, or *baken*. In marking the card, you have to decide between a win, a place, a bracket-number quinella, and a horse-number quinella. With a bracket-number quinella, if there are twelve horses in a race, they are allotted to brackets containing one or two horses. For example, there may be four brackets with two horses each and another four brackets with one horse each. If any horse in your chosen bracket comes first or second you can cash in on your bet. Horse-number quinella are sold for races where more than nine horses race and you must select the top two horses by their individual numbers, not by bracket. The odds for horse-number quinella are consequently higher and the payoffs are greater.

There are three grades of big money races in Japan. Grade One races include the Japan Cup, a 2,400 meter race over turf at the Tokyo Race Course in late November. After the Breeder's Cup Classic in Florida, the Japan Cup offers the world's biggest purse. The winner in 1992 took home 160 million yen from a total purse of 392 million yen. Another Grade One race is the Emperor's Cup, a 2,000 meter race on turf, which alternates between Kyoto and Tokyo each season.

Betting is also possible in Japan with motorboat, bicycle and motorcycle races sponsored by national, prefectural, or municipal governments.

BETTING CARD

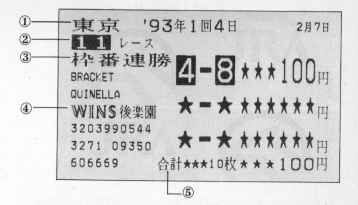

① ─ 東京 '93年1回4日　　2月7日

② ─ 11 レース

③ ─ 枠番連勝　4-8 ★★★100円
BRACKET
QUINELLA　　★-★ ★★★★★★円

④ ─ WINS後楽園
3203990544　　★-★ ★★★★★★円
3271 09350
606669　　合計★★★10枚★★★100円

└─⑤

Horse racing

① *Tōkyō '93 nen 1 kai 4 ka 2 gatsu 7 ka*
  Tokyo '93, 4th day of the 1st Series, February 7th

② *11 rēsu* 11th race

③ *Wakuban renshō 4–8 100 yen* Bracket divisions 4–8 100, yen

④ *Wins Kōrakuen* Wins Korakuen

⑤ *Gōkei 10 mai 100 yen*
  In total 10 tickets bought for 100 yen apiece

The Lottery

Does it seem to you that Lady Luck always shines on others and never on you? Perhaps it is time you tried the *takarakuji*, Japan's lotteries. For as little as three hundred yen, you could win a fortune as large as 100 million yen.

Takarakuji come in many forms. The "scratch-and-win" version is only three hundred yen. Simply use a coin to scratch off the surface printed A to F. Underneath, you'll find the winning or losing combination. In the "scratch-and-win" version, a winning combination will contain the same number three times.

You can collect your prize on the spot if it is ten thousand yen or under. If you win more than that, you will have to take the ticket to a Dai-Ichi Kangyo Bank with proof of identity. You may be quizzed on where you bought the ticket to prove it was not stolen.

Superstition frequently surrounds the purchase of a lottery ticket. Your best chances of striking it lucky is if you buy tickets at the Nishi Ginza Chance Center counter in Tokyo or the booth closest to the Karasumori exit of Shinbashi Station, also in Tokyo. Both places have reputations for providing winning tickets, but they have statistics on their sides. They both serve thousands of customers each day. Naturally the chances of selling a winning ticket are higher than those for a little old grandma selling from a booth in the middle of nowhere.

Lotteries with considerably higher rewards are regularly held around Japan. Profits usually go toward government-designated local charities or they swell the funds set aside for public work projects. These *takarakuji* tend to quickly sell out. But if you fancy beating the crowds, prepurchasing reservation tickets distributed at lottery outlets will guarantee you the chance of a small outlay on a dream.

Dating

For those whose personal connections haven't garnered a successful *omiai* or a more casual introduction, another option exists—computerized match-making agencies. Many Japanese companies with an overabundance of workers of one sex, perhaps altruistically wanting to see their employees happy, or just wanting to turn a profit on a new venture, have established such agencies. Several of these agencies have outgrown their original company origins to blossom into nation-wide networks.

The activities of some introduction agencies have even spilled over beyond the boundaries of the islands of Japan. Overseas single Japanese can enlist with some of these agencies and can arrange special package tours back to Japan for the sole purpose of meeting a selection of prospective mates. Alternatively, Japanese women who are willing to find a husband in New York or some other overseas city with a large concentration of single Japanese males can join a match-making tour with a handful of agencies.

Although some agencies only accept Japanese nationals, a few accept foreign members. In exchange for several thousand yen, a photo, and a simple questionnaire, you can peruse the personal histories and photographs of a computer-chosen selection of men or women. You can also receive counselling, advice, and invitations to social gatherings. Your membership may last a year or only several months, depending on the amount of money you are prepared to part with.

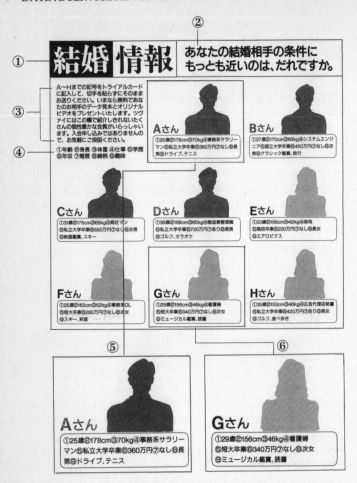

① 結婚 情報

② あなたの結婚相手の条件に もっとも近いのは、だれですか。

③ A〜Hまでの記号をトライアルカード に記入して、切手を貼らずにそのまま お送りください。いまなら無料であな たのお相手のデータ見本とオリジナル ビデオをプレゼントいたします。ツヴ ァイにはこの欄で紹介しきれないたく さんの個性豊かな会員がいらっしゃいま すので、お気軽にご投函ください。

④ ①年齢 ②身長 ③体重 ④仕事 ⑤学歴 ⑥年収 ⑦婚歴 ⑧続柄 ⑨趣味

Aさん
①25歳②178cm③70kg④事務系サラリー マン⑤私立大学卒業⑥360万円⑦なし⑧長 男⑨ドライブ、テニス

Bさん
①27歳②170cm③60kg④システムエンジ ニア⑤国立大学卒業⑥450万円⑦なし⑧次 男⑨クラシック鑑賞、旅行

Cさん
①31歳②175cm③65kg④商社マン ⑤私立大学卒業⑥550万円⑦なし⑧次男 ⑨映画鑑賞、スキー

Dさん
①38歳②168cm③65kg④製造業管理職 ⑤私立大学卒業⑥720万円⑦あり⑧長男 ⑨ゴルフ、カラオケ

Eさん
①23歳②158cm③42kg④保母 ⑤高校卒業⑥220万円⑦なし⑧長女 ⑨エアロビクス

Fさん
①25歳②162cm③52kg④事務系OL ⑤短大卒業⑥280万円⑦なし⑧次女 ⑨スキー、料理

Gさん
①29歳②156cm③46kg④看護婦 ⑤短大卒業⑥340万円⑦なし⑧次女 ⑨ミュージカル鑑賞、読書

Hさん
①35歳②153cm③46kg④広告代理店秘書 ⑤私立大学卒業⑥420万円⑦あり⑧長女 ⑨ゴルフ、食べ歩き

⑤ Aさん
①25歳②178cm③70kg④事務系サラリー マン⑤私立大学卒業⑥360万円⑦なし⑧長 男⑨ドライブ、テニス

⑥ Gさん
①29歳②156cm③46kg④看護婦 ⑤短大卒業⑥340万円⑦なし⑧次女 ⑨ミュージカル鑑賞、読書

① *Kekkon jōhō* Marriage information

② *Anata no kekkon aite no jōken ni mottomo chikai no wa dare desuka.*
Who is the closest to the marriage partner you desire?

③ *A-H made no kigō wo toraiaru-kādo ni kinyū shite, kitte wo harazu
ni sonomama ookuri kudasai. Imanara muryō de anata no oaite no
dēta mihon to orijinaru bideo wo purezento itashimasu. Tsuvai niwa
kono ran de shōkai shikirenai takusan no kosei yutakana kaiin ga
irasshaimasu. Nyūkai mōshikomi dewa arimasen node, okigaruni
gotōkan kudasai.*

Please write your selection from the choices A to H then mail
the postcard. Stamp is not required. If you mail the card in
now, we will give you a more detailed sample information
and a video of the person you selected for free. At Zwei, we
have many members with wonderful personalities that we
cannot possibly introduce in this space. Sending this card
does not mean you have made any commitment with us so
please feel free to mail it.

④ 1. *nenrei* 2. *shinchō* 3. *taijū* 4. *shigoto* 5. *gakureki* 6. *nenshū*
7. *konreki* 8. *tsuzukigara* 9. *shumi*
1. age 2. height 3. weight 4. occupation 5. academic record
6. yearly income 7. marital record 8. family relationship
9. hobbies

⑤ *A san*
1. *25 sai* 2. *178cm* 3. *70 kg* 4. *jimu-kei sararīman* 5. *shiritsu-
daigaku sotsugyō* 6. *360 man'en* 7. *nashi* 8. *chōnan* 9. *doraibu,
tenisu*
Mr. A
1. 25 years old 2. 178 cm 3. 70 kg 4. office worker 5. graduate
of a private college 6. 3.6 million yen 7.none 8. eldest son
9. driving, tennis

⑥ *G san*
1. *29 sai* 2. *156 cm* 3. *46 kg* 4. *kangofu* 5. *tandai sotsugyō* 6. *340
man'en* 7.*nashi* 8. *jijo* 9. *myūjikaru kanshō, dokusho*
Ms. G
1. 29 years old 2. 156 cm 3. 46 kg. 4. nurse 5. graduate of a
two-year college 6. 3.4 million yen 7. none 8. second daugh-
ter 9. watching musicals, reading

For Those Dangerous Liaisons

No, Passion Mint Jellies are not a type of candy. The position of this vending machine—outside a pharmacy—is a giveaway. Put your money in the slot at any time of the day or night for a pack of condoms, plain and simple for five hundred yen, lubricated for eight hundred yen, or lubricated and with jelly for a thousand yen.

Condoms are sold through vending machines, at convenience stores and pharmacies, and by door-to-door saleswomen, which explains the brief conversation I once had with a totally unknown woman who came to my door one day some years ago:

Me: Hello. May I help you?

Lady: Hello (polite smile). I wonder if I could speak to your wife.

Me: Sorry, but she's not home right now. Could I help you?

Lady: (embarrassed smile) Oh, I'm so sorry. (Backs out and closes door.)

That was the entire conversation. It took me a few moments to realize that she was not a Jehovah's Witness but had probably wanted to sell Japan's most popular form of birth control.

Around seventy-five percent of Japanese couples rely on condoms as their method of birth control. Though the birth control pill is easily the most popular method in the West, up until recently, doctors in Japan were not allowed to prescribe the pill and many Japanese women still do not know that it exists. In December 1992, the Health and Welfare Ministry found that thirty-eight of the nation's forty-seven prefectures restrict the operation of condom vending machines. The Ministry directed that the prefectures ease restrictions to make condoms more easily available to young people to prevent the spread of AIDS.

CONDOM MACHINE

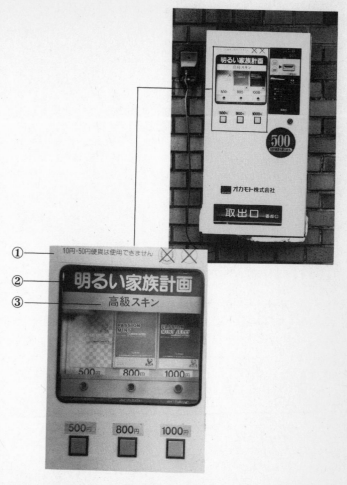

① *Jū-en gojū-en kōka wa shiyō dekimasen.*
10 yen and 50 yen coins cannot be used

② *Akarui kazoku keikaku* Cheerful family planning

③ *Kōkyū sukin* High quality condoms

Part
___
6

Culture and Customs

Shichigosan Festival

On every 15th of November, shrine grounds are sprinkled with moms and dads with video camcorders and cameras in hand, filming and photographing perfectly dressed and coifed children chasing pigeons, posing with bags of *chitose-ame* candy, or holding hands with grandma. You'll spot some spectacular tumbles in the dust as tiny three-year-old girls in kimono attempt to walk in their traditional *zōri*, or sandals. Young boys in miniature suits or *hakama*, traditional pleated pants, run in circles around their parents.

This is the date of the *Shichigosan*, the Seven-Five-Three Festival, a day when parents take their three-year-olds of either sex, or five-year-old sons or seven-year-old daughters, to the shrines to pray for their future and good health. *Shichigosan* is thought to have originated as a rite of passage. Apparently it was once believed that a newborn baby went through various stages and required several rituals performed before becoming a social entity. The *Shichigosan* itself can be traced back to seventeenth century Japan.

Why three, five, and seven? In some areas of Japan, three, five, and seven are still considered to be bad-luck years. In other areas, the odd numbers between one and nine are considered felicitous years. Whatever the answer may be, these ages were standardized as the years to take children to the shrines only relatively recently, during the nineteenth century.

During the visit, mothers and fathers buy *chitose-ame*, thousand year candy, in the happy colors of pink and white to give to the children and to distribute to relatives.

CHITOSE-AME BAG

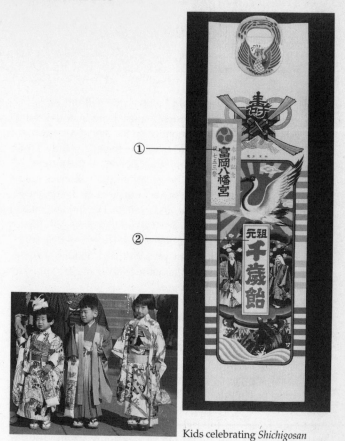

Kids celebrating *Shichigosan*

① *Sanpai kinen*
Commemoration for visiting a shrine

Tomioka Hachiman-gū
Tomioka Hachiman Shrine

Shuku Shichigosan Matsuri
Celebrate the Shichigosan Festival

② *Ganso Chitose-ame*
The original good-luck candy

Festive Fare

No festival in Japan would be the same without *yatai*, the open-air stalls that suddenly mushroom in and around the precincts of shrines and temples on the day of a festival. In summer and autumn it is hard to escape them, given the large number of festivals that occupy the calender at these times of the year. The *yatai* sell everything: cotton candy, bonsai, goldfish, cute little chicks that die in a day, ancient medicinal cures of dubious origin, masks, toys, and even kitchen implements.

The most ubiquitous *yatai* are the vendors of *takoyaki* (octopus fritters), *kōri* (snow cones), *okonomiyaki* (Japanese-style spicy omelettes), *ramune* (soda) and *yakisoba* (fried noodles). These five are the mainstays of any Japanese festival and are sure fire moneymakers for the stall keepers.

While most people in Japan happily frequent festivals and devour their *takoyaki* or *yakisoba* washed down with *ramune*, many are blissfully unaware that the *yatai* operators, or *tekiya*, in many instances are also an important branch of the nation's network of gangsters, *yakuza*. *Tekiya* who work at festivals organize their own place-allocation gatherings one or two days before the start of a festival. The place allotted to each *tekiya's* stall can have a big bearing on his income. The top moneymaking locations are on the right as you face a shrine or temple. Japanese tend to walk on the left as they approach and leave a shrine or temple. Every *tekiya* knows that it is on their way out that potential customers will be in a money-spending mood—even if the *yakisoba* is overdone, the *ramune* is lukewarm, or the *takoyaki* is a bit short on octopus.

①

②

④

③

① *Meibutsu, Anzu ame, Chinmi*
Local specialty, Candied apricot, Exotic taste

② *Tokusei, Aji-jiman, Yakisoba, Tokusei*
Specially-made, Best-tasting, Stir-fried noodles, Specially-made

③ *Aji-jiman, Tokusei, Okonomiyaki*
Best-tasting, Specially-made, Japanese-style omelette

④ *Hiyashi ramune* Cold soda

Rice

My local rice vendor assures me that Japan imports foreign rice. "It's just that nobody realizes that rice crackers and some noodles already contain foreign rice," he says. But he also says that foreign rice has a bad image to overcome in Japan. According to him, after the war, Japanese had to eat American rice because they were hungry. Now, even though Japanese rice is four or five times the world price, it's still the sort of rice the Japanese like to eat.

He has a point. The Japanese government has established numerous rice testing centers around the country dedicated to producing rice types suited to the Japanese palate as well as to the different climatic regions in Japan. The result is a wide range of rice types which my local rice vendor assures me are liked by millions of loyal Japanese consumers.

At the top end of the market is *koshihikari* rice. This type of rice is reputedly among the best in Japan because of its propensity to retain moisture and remain fluffy long after being cooked. Niigata prefecture claims to grow the best *koshihikari* rice because its rice is grown in valleys which heat up during the day and are cold at night, creating the perfect temperature differential necessary to produce good rice. Fukushima prefecture also claims its rice is the best. Its Adatara rice, named after the nearby Adatara mountains, is grown with a minimum of chemicals and lots of natural fertilizers. At the bottom end of the market is government stockpiled rice which may have been sitting in a granary for up to three years before being sold. Old rice loses its propensity to absorb and retain moisture.

A BAG OF *KOSHIHIKARI* RICE (FRONT AND BACK)

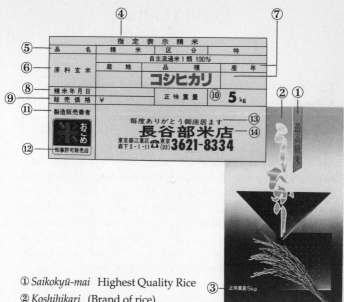

① *Saikokyū-mai* Highest Quality Rice

② *Koshihikari* (Brand of rice)

③ *Shōmijūryō 5 kg* Net Weight 5 kg

④ *Shitei hyōji seimai* Standard form for polished rice

⑤ *Hinmei: seimai, Kubun: toku*
Type of rice: polished rice, Class: excellent

⑥ *Genryō genmai: jishu-ryūtsūmai 1 rui 100%* Grade of unpolished
rice: semi-rationed rice, 100% first class

⑦ *Sanchi __, Hinshu: Koshihikari, Sannen __* Place produced __,
Type of rice: koshihikari, Year produced __

⑧ *Seimai nengappi__* Date rice was polished__

⑨ *Hanbai kakaku__* Sales price__

⑩ *Shōmijūryo: 5kg* Net Weight: 5 kg

⑪ *Seizō-hanbai-gyōsha* Production sales trade

⑫ *Chiji kyoka-hanbai-ten* Sales licensed by the Governor

⑬ *Madio arigatō gozaimasu.* Thank you very much.

⑭ *Hasebe Kome-ten* Hasebe Rice Store

Giving Gifts

I once wrote about a day in the life of a group of Japanese tourists in Australia. They arrived at Sydney airport barely awake, after being up half the night spotting penguins at a beach near Melbourne. As soon as they got in the bus which took them to all the sights—the beaches, the harbor and the opera house—most of them fell asleep. At each place they tumbled out, took photos, and returned to their seats to sleep. But at the last stop, a duty-free shop, I witnessed a transformation. As the guide announced their arrival, people stirred, heads bobbed up, wives nudged their sleeping husbands. The moment they were all waiting for had arrived—their chance to stock up on gifts for the folks back home. Their buying frenzy lasted thirty minutes longer than the allotted time.

Omiyage, gifts brought back from your travels, are part of the Japanese cult of journeying. Not to bring back *omiyage* for friends, colleagues, or relatives is a serious break with etiquette. *Omiyage* chocolates and candy are a way of thanking those who took over your responsibilities while you were away and granted you time off for a few days.

Omiyage are part of a larger gift-giving culture in Japan. Most large department stores have an entire floor of pre-packaged gifts to support this culture. People give small gifts when they visit someone's home, when someone does them a favor, or when someone introduces them to someone else. There are two established gift-giving seasons during which one distributes these gifts, one at the end of July and the other at the end of the year. Gifts in the summer are called *ochūgen*. Those given at year-end are called *oseibo*. Typical gifts include coupons for department store purchases, canned goods, beer, and household items such as towels, soap, and shampoo.

Lantern in front of stores selling
Shogōin Yatsuhashi

① *Shogōin Yatsuhashi* (Brand name of cinnamon cookie)

Getting Married

Has Cupid's arrow struck you in Japan? Do you want to get married? As a non-Japanese, tying the knot with a Japanese spouse involves red tape.

No couple in Japan is recognized as legally married until they register with the local ward or town office by filling out a *kon'in todoke*, a notification of marriage. Before the form can be filled out, your Japanese partner must submit an official copy of his or her family register, *koseki tōhon*. You, the non-Japanese partner, must submit a number of items: your passport, an alien registration certificate, a certificate showing that this registration has been filed in the ward where you live, and a *kon'in gubi shōmeisho*, a document affirming that you have the legal status to marry. This should be issued by your diplomatic office in Japan and should be translated into Japanese. Finally, if you are a Taiwanese or North or South Korean who wishes to marry a Japanese national, you must submit a copy of your family register as well.

When filling out the notification of marriage, in the section where the Japanese partner writes in his or her *honseki*, or registered domicile, you should write in your nationality. In so doing, your name and nationality rate a mention on the Japanese spouse's *honseki*.

One additional fact. When two Japanese marry, the law obliges them to take a single family name. Most opt for the husband's name. But with a marriage involving one non-Japanese, separate family names can be retained.

LEGAL MARRIAGE NOTIFICATION FORM

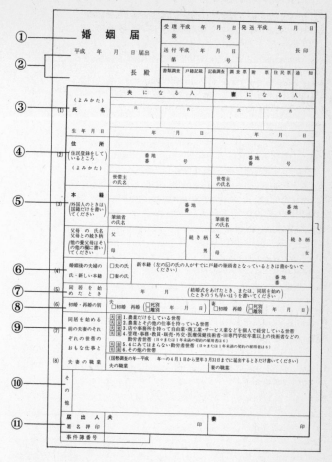

① *Kon'in todoke*
Notification of marriage

② *Heisei __nen __gatsu __nichi todokede*
Heisei __year __month __day notified

__*chō dono*
To Ward Chief __

③ 1. *(Yomikata), Shimei, Seinen gappi*
(Reading), Name, Date of birth

④ 2. *Jūsho, (Jūmin-tōroku wo shiteiru tokoro), (Yomikata)*
Address, (Please write registered place of present
domicile), (Reading)

⑤ 3. *Honseki, (Gaikokujin no toki wa kokuseki dake wo
kaitekudasai.)*
Registered permanent domicile, (In the case of a
foreign national, please write down nationality
only.)

*Fubo no shimei, Fubo to no tsuzukigara, (Ta no yōfubo
wa sonota no ran ni kaitekudasai.)*
Name of parents, Relation to parent [i.e. second
son], (If parents are not biological parents, then
please write on a separate line.)

⑥ 4. *Kon'in go no fūfu no shi • atarashii honseki*
Surname • new registered permanent domicile of
couples once married

⑦ 5. *Dōkyo wo hajimeta toki*
When started to live together

⑧ 6. *Shokon • saikon no betsu*
First marriage • remarriage

⑨ 7. *Dōkyo wo hajimeru mae no fusai no sorezore no setai
no omona shigoto to fusai no shokugyō*
Before living together, the main occupation of the
couple and/or their family

⑩ *Sonota* Other

⑪ *Todokedenin, Shomei ouin*
Names of those applying for marriage, Stamp of
personal seal

Weddings

Go to a wedding in Japan and you won't come back empty-handed. You will receive a *hikidemono*, a parting gift from the newlyweds, as thanks for attending the wedding. This could be anything from four thousand yen soup bowls to a twenty-five thousand yen jewelry box, but increasingly it tends to be more readily consumable items such as high quality chocolates or tea.

Of course, in the gift-giving culture of Japan, wedding etiquette requires that you, as guests, take along a gift of cash as well. How close you are with the newlyweds and your age usually determines the amount of money you give. As a rough guide, you won't be off the mark if you give twenty to thirty thousand yen. Though the amount of cash that is customarily given may surprise you as being exorbitant, weddings in Japan are horrendously expensive. It is commonly said that it would be cheaper for a couple to transport their immediate family to Hawaii for a wedding ceremony than to have a ceremony in Japan. Your gift of cash should be enclosed in special envelopes called *shūgi bukuro*, which you can purchase at department stores, stationery stores, or even convenience stores. Put the cash inside and be sure to write the amount of cash you have enclosed on the back of the inner envelope and your name on the front of the outer envelope.

Shinto weddings usually involve only the immediate family and a *nakōdo*, the go-between. So don't be upset if you are not asked to the actual wedding. In modern Japanese hotel or marriage-hall wedding ceremonies, many rituals and events symbolizing the union of two people are held for all to enjoy. You may even be asked to actively participate by making a short speech, so brush up on your Japanese.

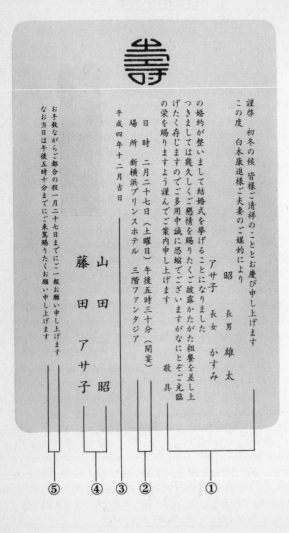

謹啓　初冬の候　皆様ご清祥のこととお慶び申し上げます

この度　白木康進様ご夫妻のご媒妁により

　　　　　　　　　昭　長男　雄　太

　　アサ子　長女　かすみ

の婚約が整いまして結婚式を挙げることになりました

つきましては幾久しくご懇情を賜りたくご披露かたがた粗餐を差し上

げたく存じますのでご多用中誠に恐縮でございますがなにとぞご光臨

の栄を賜りますよう謹んでご案内申し上げます

　　　　　　　　　　　　　　　　　　　　　敬具

平成四年十二月吉日

　日　時　二月二十七日（土曜日）午後五時三十分（開宴）

　場　所　新横浜プリンスホテル　三階ファンタジア

　　　　　山　田　　　昭

　　　藤　田　アサ子

お手数ながらご都合の程一月二十七日までにご一報お願い申し上げます

なお当日は午後五時十分までにご来駕賜りたくお願い申し上げます

①　②　③　④　⑤

130

① *Kinkei. Shotō no kō minasama goseishō no koto to oyorokobi mōshiagemasu. Konotabi Shiraki Kōshin sama gofusai no gobaishaku ni yori*
   Akira chōnan Yūta
   Asako chōjo Kasumi
*no kon'yaku ga totonoimashite kekkonshiki wo ageru koto ni nari-
mashita. Tsukimashite wa ikuhisashiku gokonjō wo tamawaritaku
gohirō katagata sosan wo sashiagetaku zonjimasu node gotayōchū
makotoni kyōshuku de gozaimasu ga nanitozo gokōrin no ei wo
tamawarimasu yō tsutsushinde goannai mōshiagemasu.*
The beginning of winter has arrived. We trust that everyone is
well and prospering. On this occasion, through the match-making of Mr. and Mrs. Shiraki Koshin, we would like to announce
the marriage of Akira's first son, Yuta and Asako's first daugh-
ter, Kasumi. In hopes for your continued favor, we would like to
hold a reception with a meal. We are sorry to disturb you at such
a busy time but if you can, please join us.

② *Nichiji: ni gatsu nijū-shichi nichi (doyōbi), Gogo go ji sanjū pun (kaien)*
Time/date: February 27th (Saturday), 5:30 P.M. (opening)

Basho: Shin-Yokohama Purinsu Hoteru san-gai fantajia
Place: Shin-Yokohama Prince Hotel 3rd Flr Fantasia [Hall]

③ *Heisei yo nen jūnigatsu kichijitsu*
Heisei 4 December 12 Lucky Day [for announcing the wedding]

④ *Yamada Akira*
Fujita Asako
(Name of those making the announcement. In this case, they are
the father of the groom and the mother of the bride.)

⑤ *Otesū nagara gotsugō no hodo ichigatsu nijūshichi nichi made ni goip-
pō onegai mōshiagemasu. Nao tōjitsu wa gogo go-ji juppun made ni
goraiga tamawaritaku onegai mōshiagemasu.*
It would be greatly appreciated if you could give a reply by January 27th. We ask that you come by 5:10 P.M. to the hall.

A ritual Shinto-style wedding ceremony

131

Way of the Gods

Often, while walking around in Japan, you come across red gates, called *torii*, or straw ropes with dangling white papers enclosing a tree or stone. Both of these items indicate the presence of a natural object or phenomena that is considered powerful or sacred. The ropes enclose a *kami*, while behind the *torii* is a shrine dedicated to or housing a *kami*. *Kami* are the deities of the Shinto religion, Japan's indigenous religion.

Shinto comprises various rites, festivals, and beliefs stemming from basic desires, such as the need for food, protection from natural forces, and a concern about purity and defilement. Though Shinto was originally connected to the rice cultivation culture of Japan, it has withstood Japan's urbanization. Many homes still have a house altar for the *kami* that protect their occupants; a ritual is performed by priests everytime a new building is put up in Tokyo.

Ise Shrine in Mie Prefecture, the main Shinto shrine, enshrines the goddess, Amaterasu Omikami. According to Shinto mythology, the Imperial family is descended from Amaterasu. Imperial family members still go to Ise Shrine to pay their respects. Soon after Crown Prince Naruhito and Crown Princess Masako married, they went to Ise Shrine to report their marriage to the ancestral gods and goddess. The goddess is represented by a sacred mirror which is part of the imperial regalia. However, don't think that if you go, you'll be able to see Amaterasu's manifestation. It is kept in the inner sanctum, locked away from all eyes. Every twenty years, an elaborate ceremony occurs when the Goddess is transferred from the inner shrine to a new inner shrine built in the same form in an adjoining plot. The first inner shrine was said to have originated in the third century. The next rebuilding will occur in 1994.

Ise Jingu Shrine

① *Dai rokujū-ikkai Ise Jingū shikinen sengū ni hōsan itashimashō.*
Let's revere the sixty-first ritual rebuilding at Ise Shrine.

② *Yomigaeru Nihon no kokoro gosengū.*
Reviving the spirit of Japan. Rebuilding the shrine.

③ *Ise Jingū shikinen sengū hōsan kai Tōkyō-to honbu*
Tokyo headquarters for the Society for Revering the Rebuilding Ritual at Ise Shrine

Tōkyō-to Jinja-chō Tokyo Agency Shrine

Tōkyō-to Jinja Sōdai-kai Tokyo Shrine Representative Society

Funerals

Those attending funerals customarily contribute a condolence gift of cash, a *kōden*. Funerals can be costly for family members; the average funeral in Japan is estimated to cost about a million yen. So your *kōden* of about five to ten thousand yen is a way of helping out the deceased's family.

You should place your *kōden* in a *bushūgi bukuro*, a funeral envelope. Write the amount enclosed on the inner envelope and your name on the outer envelope. Offer your envelope to the receptionist at the entrance of the funeral hall or home.

At funeral services, men traditionally wear black suits teamed with black ties. Women going to funerals almost uniformly wear black dresses with simple pearl necklaces. If you are attending the *otsuya*, or the wake, a bowl of incense will be passed around during the praying. When it comes to you, pick up a pinch of incense with your thumb, index, and middle fingers, raise it to your forehead, and then place it in the bowl. Repeat this action one more time and then pass the incense to the person next to you. If you are attending the *sōgi*, the Buddhist funeral rites, stand in line to offer incense at the altar. When your turn comes, bow to the family and priest as you pass the body and then bow at the altar and offer incense as one does at a wake.

Don't be surprised when about ten days later you receive, by special delivery, a package from the family containing some useful household item or a package of assorted teas. This is their way of expressing thanks to you for coming to the funeral and offering your support.

③ ② ①

Sign on left indicates where funeral service will be held. Sign on right tells dates and time of mourning services and is placed on door of deceased person's house.

① *Tsuya __gatsu __nichi __ji yori.*
   Wake begins at __month___day __time.

② *Yasunari-ke sōgi shikijō*
   Hall for funeral services for the Yasunari family

③ *Kokubetsushiki san gatsu nijūgo nichi jūsan ji yori*
   Funeral Service at 13:00, March 25

Minding Your Manners

Many signs in subway stations consist of warnings against standing too close to the edge of the platform, standing in the way of large numbers of passengers alighting from or boarding trains, and smoking during rush hour. Since 1974, Tokyo subway passengers have also had their days brightened by a series of monthly posters appealing to them to display a better standard of manners toward their fellow passengers. Known as "manner posters," these posters exhort passengers not to forget their umbrellas, sprawl on seats with their legs sticking out, or put their luggage on the seats next to them.

Recently, the Teito Rapid Transit used famous Japanese actors and television personalities. Personalities were chosen on the basis of their *seiketsukan*, or wholesomeness, and popularity. The list of personalities used includes golfer Yuko Moriguchi, Takarazuka all-female review star Rei Asami, the heavily made-up actor-singer, Yoshiki, from the rock group "X," the former baseball player Shigeru Takada, and actor Masato Hagiwara.

The publicity department claims that manners have improved in Tokyo's subways over the past decade and it credits the posters for this. The most popular poster in the recent series was one showing actor-singer Yoshiki. The all-time most popular poster was one used during the rainy season one year, depicting Marilyn Monroe in a scene from the movie *River of No Return*. The poster's theme was "umbrellas of no return," and it referred to the large number of umbrellas which are left on trains during the rainy season.

① *Nonbiri ofu, shikkari on.*
Let's relax during our time off, and be on the ball at work!

② *Yoyū de itte, baribari shigoto, baribari benkyō. Jisa tsūkin tsūgaku ni gokyōryoku kudasai.*
Please go with time to spare, and then work hard, study hard. Please cooperate by staggering your commute to work or school from the rush hour.

③ *Manā postā* Manner poster

New Year's Cards

J ust when you surface for a breath after writing all of your Christmas cards, you are hit with the annual Japanese chore of writing *nengajō*, or New Year's cards. *Nengajō* came into vogue late last century as an adjunct to the Japanese custom of paying New Year's visits. They take care of all the people you cannot possibly manage to visit in the three or four days before getting back to work.

When sending out New Year's cards, be sure to use *nengajō*, not normal postcards. A *nengajō* has a special imprint below the stamp indicating that it is a New Year's card. When mail sorters see this imprint, they wait to deliver it until January 1st.

Two types of *nengajō* are available. The 41 yen *nengajō* are the same price as normal postcards and are available at the post office and at stores. The post office also issues a postcard that costs a few more yen. These extra yen are given as a donation to a government-designated charity.

If you score even one *nengajō* this year, hold on to it; it could be valuable. Certain types of *nengajō* available at the post office could win you an *otoshidama*. *Otoshidama* are normally small amounts of money given to children during the first few days of January; however, in this case, it is a prize you win if you hold the *nengajō* with a winning combination of numbers. Your *nengajō's* numbers are on the bottom of the postcard. The winners of the *otoshidama* are selected every year on January 15th. A Japanese archer strikes a rotating dartboard to select the winning numbers for the *nengajō* lottery. This event is broadcast live on television. If you miss the telecast, the winning numbers are available from your nearest post office. Prizes include televisions, bicycles, microwave ovens, stationery sets, and stamps.

①

②

③

④

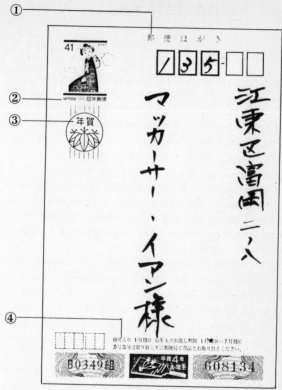

郵便はがき

Nengajō sent to the author

① *Yūbin hagaki* Postcard

② *Nippon 1992 Nihon Yūbin* Japan 1992 Japan Mail

③ *Nenga* New Year's Greetings

④ *Chūsenbi 1 gatsu 15 nichi. Otoshidama no owatashi-kikan 1 gatsu 16 nichi–7 gatsu 16 nichi. Bangō bubun wo kiritorazu ni yūbinkyoku de shōhin to otorikae-kudasai.*
Lottery day is January 15. Prizes available from January 16 to July 16. Please exchange the card with numbered section intact for your prize at a post office.

The New Year

At midnight on New Year's Eve, the feeling of peace and tranquility generated by the sound of a distant temple bell can be a profoundly moving experience, especially if you are in a place such as Kyoto or Kamakura, where temples seem to surround you like the hills around those cities. Despite the rush to destroy and rebuild that grips the country for most of the year, the New Year's holiday seems to be a time when Japan recalls its traditions. Even imitation leather-jacketed bikers and their gals line up with the rest of the crowd for the annual trooping of the colors on *hatsumōde*, the first visit in the new year to a shrine or temple to pray for happiness and good fortune during the coming year.

In Tokyo, giggling girls in kimono and their self-conscious boyfriends, bank clerks, futures traders, moms, dads, and babies all brave packed late night trains to join the crowd of thousands heading for Meiji Shrine, one of Tokyo's main Shinto centers of worship. At Meiji Shrine, the crowd is so dense that temporary traffic lights are erected within the shrine precincts.

After praying for the New Year, worshippers may purchase a number of items. One is a *hamaya*, an arrow that symbolizes the wish to travel straight and true through the coming year. An *omamori*, a talisman, can bring good fortune, good health, or entrance into a top university. Another purchase is an *omikuji*, an oracle or fortune written on a small slip of paper. From the possibility of receiving small, medium, or big good luck, I scored a "small good luck" *omikuji*. If you don't like what you get in the draw, it is the custom to tie the *omikuji* to the branch of a tree by the temple or shrine where it was purchased, in hope that the gods will protect you from a bad future.

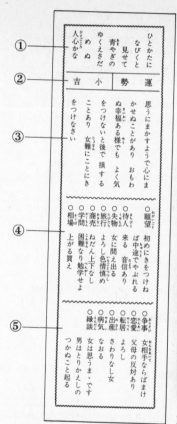

Omikuji tied to a tree at Tomioka Hachiman shrine

① ひとかたに
なびくと
見せて
青やぎの
ゆくえさだ
め
ぬ
人心かな

② 運勢　小吉

③ 思うにまかすように心にまかせぬことがあり おもわぬ幸福ある様でも よく気をつけないと後で 損することあり 女難にことにきをつけなさい

④
○顧望　初めにきをつけねば中途でやぶれる
○待人　来る 音信あり
○失物　女に問え出る
○旅行　よろし色情慎め
○商売　だん上下なし
○学問　困難なり勉学せよ
○相場　上がる買え

⑤
○争事　女相手ならばまけ
○恋愛　父母の反対あり
○転居　よろし
○出産　さわりなし女
○病気　なおる
○縁談　女は思うま、です　男はとりかえしのつかぬこと起る

① [Japanese on the *omikuji* is to be read from the right to left]
Hito kata ni nabiku to misete aoyagi no yukue sadamenu hitogokoro kana.

The movement of the mind, like the free willow bending—uncertain

② *Unsei: shōkichi*
Fortune: small good luck

③ *Omou ni makasu yōde kokoro ni makasenu koto ga ari. Omowanu sai-*
wai aru yōdemo, yoku ki wo tsukenai to, ato de son suru koto ari. Jonan
ni koto ni ki wo tsukenasai.

Something may be settled in your mind but things may not
work out. You may appear to encounter unexpected good fortune, but if you do not remain on your guard, there will be a loss
later. Be on your guard against problems with women.

④ *Negaigoto: Hajime ni ki wo tsukeneba chūto de yabureru.*
Wishes: If you are not cautious at the beginning your wish will
be broken along the way.

Machibito: Kitaru. Tayori ari.
Someone you are waiting for: Will arrive. There is a letter.

Usemono: Onna ni toe, deru.
Something lost: You'll find it if you ask a woman.

Tabidachi: Yoroshi, irogoto tsutsushime.
Starting on a journey: Fine. Exercise caution love.

Akinai: Nedan jōge nashi.
Business: No price movement up or down.

Gakumon: Konnan nari, bengakuseyo.
Study: There will be difficulties. Study hard.

Sōba: Agaru, kae.
The stock exchange: Will go up. Buy!

⑤ *Arasoi: Onna aite naraba make.*
Struggles: You will be defeated if your opponent is a woman.

Ren'ai: Fubo no hantai ari.
Love affair: Opposition from parents.

Yautsuri: Yoroshi.
Moving home: Fine.

Osan: sawari nashi, onna.
Birth: Girl born with no problems

Yamai: Naoru.
Sickness: You will be cured.

Endan: Onna wa omou mama desu. Otoko wa torikaeshi no tsukanu
koto okoru.
Marriage proposals: Will work as a woman wishes. A man will
encounter something irrevocable.

NUMBERS

1	*ichi*
2	*ni*
3	*san*
4	*shi* or *yon*
5	*go*
6	*roku*
7	*shichi* or *nana*
8	*hachi*
9	*kyū* or *ku*
10	*jū*
100	*hyaku*
1,000	*sen*
10,000	*ichiman*

DATES

the 1st (of March)	*(san gatsu) tsuitachi*
the 2nd	*futsuka*
the 3rd	*mikka*
the 4th	*yokka*
the 5th	*itsuka*
the 6th	*muika*
the 7th	*nanoka*
the 8th	*yōka*
the 9th	*kokonoka*
the 10th	*tōka*
the 14th	*jūyokka*
the 20th	*hatsuka*

IAN McARTHUR: Born in 1950, Ian McArthur studied Japanese language at Queensland University and Keio University's International Center and has spent a total of more than 10 years in Japan. He is the author of two Kodansha International books on colloquial expressions in the English and Japanese and another Kodansha volume on the Australian-born traditional Japanese comic storyteller Henry (Kairaku-toi) Black. Ian McArthur works as a journalist and translator for the International Department at Kyodo News Service in Tokyo.